Domestic Labour Problems and their Solution

In these days of Rationed Gas and Domestic Servant shortage, problems arising therefrom can only be solved by Mechanical Aids. The Appliances here featured have proved their worth, and each undoubtedly solves the problem to which it applies. They are being readily adopted in every home that has for its aim the Elimination of Drudgery, and the attainment of the highest degree of Domestic Efficiency.

WE PREACH

The Gospel of Domestic Efficiency, of the emancipation of woman from the shackles of domestic drudgery, and we are **Acknowledged Experts.**

The "NATIONAL ECONOMY" Cooker

was put on the market to cope with the coal crisis. The "National Economy" Cooker does all your cooking with the use of ONLY ONE gas ring. The heat is conserved and regulated, and you not only economise in the use of gas, but you prevent Food Wastage, and make cooking a real pleasure - - - **45/-**

WE INVITE

you to get in touch with us on any problem affecting your domestic labour Inquire from us on all matters appertaining to Domestic Science.

"REDSTAR" Washing Machine

does the work better in half the time, and the clothes last longer than when treated by the laundry. Cannot tear the clothes. Machine-cut gears on ball-bearings give it the running ease of a bicycle, and it requires much less energy to operate than a sewing machine. - **£8.0.0**

THE ELECTRIC "SWEEPER-VAC"

with its gently tapping, fast-turning, motor-driven brush not only removes every speck of lint, hair, embedded dirt from rugs and carpets, but also cleans hard wood floors, linoleum, upholstery, mattresses and stairs. Brush is under independent control. The Electric Sweeper-Vac is light in weight, simple to handle and economical in use, and by virtue of its exclusive patented features and sound construction, presents a Cleaner that has been brought to the highest state of mechanical perfection - - - **£18.18.0**

The Famous "PNEUVAC DO-ALL" Bucket and Mop

Enables you to wash floors without kneeling. Hands do not come in contact with the water, which permits you to use boiling water and the strongest disinfectants. Ideal for washing down outhouses, and domestic use, tile floors, linoleums, etc. Strong and well made. Be sure it is the "PNEUVAC DO-ALL" Outfit - **13/6**

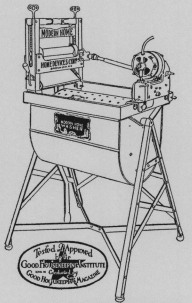
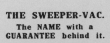

THE SWEEPER-VAC.

The NAME with a GUARANTEE behind it.

Is like no other machine. It is the machine that completely cleanses a carpet in one process. "SWEEPS & SUCTION CLEANS" without the aid of electricity.

The ONLY Three-in-One Machine in the World.

The principle on which it is constructed and operated has undoubted advantages over all other methods of carpet-cleaning. It embraces Three Distinct Machines, which can be used in combination or separately - -

THE "MODERN HOME" WASHER

does all the washing, rinsing, wringing, and blueing by electricity—without work, with less soap, much quicker, better, cleaner, and at less expense than when done at the laundry. Clothes will last six times as long when done by the "Modern Home." The ordinary domestic wash takes about an hour, at the cost of 1d. for current. The "Modern Home" soon pays for itself in these days of high laundry bills, and will last a lifetime. - £12.10.0

"DOMESTIC LOG...
careful and discerning housew... ...matters of utmost interest to the ...postcard. **WRITE NOW.**

THE LONDON ... ...PANY, LIMITED, 267, High Holborn ... *Telephone:* HOLBORN 158.

DAILY MAIL - IDEAL HOME EXHIBITION

The Ideal Home

THROUGH THE 20TH CENTURY

Lord Northcliffe, founder of the Daily Mail, in 1897

DAILY MAIL - IDEAL HOME EXHIBITION

The Ideal Home

THROUGH THE 20TH CENTURY

DEBORAH S. RYAN

HAZAR
P·U·B·L·I·S·H·I·N·G

For my Grandparents
Rob and Nora Roberts

Text copyright © Deborah S. Ryan 1997
Volume copyright © Hazar Publishing 1997

Published in 1997 by
Hazar Publishing Ltd.
147 Chiswick High Road, London W4 2DT

Edited by Marie Clayton
Designed by John Dunne
Printed and bound by Butler & Tanner, England

A catalogue record for this title is available from the British Library

ISBN 1 874371 81 4

Contents

Foreword

The twentieth century has seen the blossoming of the love affair between the British and their homes. At the turn of the century, home-making was perceived by most as an uninspiring exercise, usually driven by utilitarian necessity. The generally low levels of income were hardly conducive to changing this viewpoint. To spend what little spare money there was on the domestic environment would have been regarded by most as eccentric, to say the least.

But then things changed and the last 100 years has witnessed a radical re-appraisal in our attitudes towards our home. The purely functional is no longer acceptable. Home-making has become a glamorous pursuit, a national passion that more and more people have been able to indulge as we enjoyed ever greater prosperity.

The Daily Mail Ideal Home Exhibition has played a major part in this huge cultural shift. Since its inception in 1908, the Exhibition has not merely mirrored the explosion of interest in home-making, it has been at the forefront in influencing public taste. Indeed, the Exhibition established itself as a 3-dimensional advice manual, its founders recognising that few possessed the gift to create an "ideal home" unaided. Although it has spawned many imitators in its long and prestigious history, the Ideal Home Exhibition remains the touchstone for what is innovative and fashionable in the realm of home-making.

To revisit the Ideal Home Exhibitions of the past is to gain a fascinating insight into the changing background of our social history. As an example, the literature accompanying the 1910 Exhibition boldly claimed that "No home can really be ideal unless it contains at least one man, one woman and, if possible, one baby, or else a good substitute".

These pages embrace a century of social attitudes, technological developments and design innovations. But they do more than that. For the Ideal Home Exhibition has always represented an aspirational world, a world far enough removed to be spectacular, yet close enough to be attainable. As such, this book captures the hopes and dreams of ordinary people from Edwardian times to the present day.

SIR DAVID ENGLISH
CHAIRMAN AND EDITOR-IN-CHIEF
ASSOCIATED NEWSPAPERS

Acknowledgements

This book has been researched and written with a great deal of practical support
and intellectual stimulation. I am grateful to Meg Sweet and Jan van der Wateren of the
Victoria and Albert Museum, who encouraged me to start this research. I would like to thank
my PhD supervisors in the Department of Cultural Studies at the University of East London -
Sally Alexander, Mica Nava and Alan O'Shea - as well as my examiners Bill Schwarz,
Penny Sparke and Elizabeth Wilson. I am grateful to the encouragement and suggestions of
those who read and listened to my work in progress: especially Andrew Blake,
Christopher Breward, John Carey, Fan Carter, Claire Catterall, Alison Clarke, Felix Driver,
Graham Evans, David Gilbert, Paul Greenhalgh, Julian Holder, Alison Light, Maggie Moran
and Raphael Samuel. I am also grateful to my former colleagues and students in the
History of Art and Design Departments of the University of Wolverhampton and the
University of East London, and the Geography Department of Royal Holloway,
University of London.

I am grateful to everyone at Associated Newspapers, in particular Paul Rossiter,
Dave Sheppard, Brian Jackson and Alan Pinnock for their encouragement and for providing
archive material. Thanks also to Bob Dignum and his predecessors for maintaining the quality
of the archive through the 20th century. Without their dedication this book would not have
been possible. Special thanks to Steve Torrington, who insisted that my PhD thesis should be
published in this form for a wider audience. I am also grateful to Vyvyan Harmsworth,
who kindly answered my questions. I would like to thank Nick James and his colleagues at
D.M.G. Exhibitions Group Limited for access to their records, and Victor Bryant of
Earls Court Olympia Limited. Members of the Exhibition Study Group, especially Bill Tonkin,
have been enthusiastic, helpful and supplied the postcard illustrations. Mike Carter has been
generous with his memories, as have Lady Elizabeth Brunner and Virginia Royds.
Thanks to Marie Clayton, who edited my thesis and added much information for the later
years. Thanks also to John Dunne for the design, to Mark Brown for help with the layouts
and T.E.H. Publishing for their editorial input.

Finally, I am deeply grateful to my family and friends for their support and encouragement
for this project over several years. Furthermore, this book would never have been completed
if it were not for my husband, James Ryan - for his intellectual engagement,
endless encouragement and love.

Introduction

From its very beginning in 1908, the Daily Mail Ideal Home Exhibition has been a major influence on the public's taste in all matters that make a house a home. Through a unique combination of educational, entertaining and hard commercial features, it has been immensely popular and appealing, promoting a modern way of life and helping to establish a culture of home-making. It has not just been an exhibition of the latest labour-saving appliances, but also entertained and educated its audience with nostalgic features, exciting forecasts of housing of the future, historical tableaux showing how home-making has advanced and interesting anthropological displays of other Peoples' homes.

The Ideal Home Exhibition was originally founded in 1908 by Wareham Smith, Advertising Manager of the Daily Mail, as a publicity tool and a way of increasing advertising revenue. In his autobiography Wareham Smith claimed that the Exhibition led the way in showing the art of home-making. It was specifically English, rather then British - from 1931 separate Scottish Ideal Home Exhibitions were held in Glasgow. The Daily Mail itself had been launched in May 1896 by Lord Northcliffe, whilst still Alfred Harmsworth, to appeal to the new mass market created by the spread of literacy. It was planned to appeal to the literate middle classes with disposable income, and particularly to clerks, claiming that its page size was handy for commuters. Northcliffe also saw women readers as a great potential market for newspapers and he incorporated a special magazine page for them. At the end of the First World War he also appointed Mrs C.S. Peel, a well-known expert on domestic matters, as Editor of the Women's page and the newspaper benefited greatly from her expertise on household management and knowledge of new labour-saving ideas. Mrs Peel felt that Northcliffe and the Daily Mail understood the needs of intelligent women, whilst other newspapers expected them only to be interested in knitting jumpers, caring for their complexions, looking after babies, cooking and in silly stories about weddings.

The Daily Mail did not merely reflect the world in which its readers lived; it also presented an aspirational world into which readers could project themselves. It was a great success, since it extended the news beyond the traditional areas of politics and business by reporting on mundane features of daily life or what became known as 'human interest' stories. The ideal audience that Northcliffe had identified for the Daily Mail was integral to the later success of the Ideal Home Exhibition.

The Special Publicity Department

Wareham Smith, Advertising Manager of the Daily Mail and Head of the Special Publicity Department, was a pioneer in the development of newspaper advertising. Born in 1874, Smith joined the Daily Mail as an advertising clerk when it was founded in 1896. He worked his way up, becoming a director of Associated Newspapers, publishers of the Daily Mail, in 1907. Smith experimented with more exciting newspaper layouts, breaking columns with advertisements and using large type. Lord Northcliffe did not always appreciate Smith's

Above: Celebrities of stage and screen were eager to visit the Exhibition, either to publicise their latest venture or in connection with charity. Miss Dorothy Ward, who was a well-known actress in the twenties, sells tickets for the Hospital Charities' Ballot at the 1927 Exhibition.

endeavours and was particularly disturbed by the inroads that advertisements made into the news columns, as was recalled by Tom Clarke, one of the Daily Mail's editors:

'You are killing the news,' he would say. 'I have instructed the advertising department to take out any of your bludgeoning advertisements. I want to encourage advertising, but I will not perform Byzantine genuflections before it.'

Despite Northcliffe's misgivings, Smith introduced other innovations, as he recalled in his 1922 autobiography, Spilt Ink:

One of the most useful organisations I began at Carmelite House was the Special Publicity Department. Its functions were to create special inducements to secure advertisements from people who did not advertise to any extent.

With a staff of fourteen, including seven canvassers and an editorial writer, the Department cost about £70 a week to run, but generated an annual turnover in 1907-8 of £26,000. Smith appointed Frederick Moir Bussy to manage the Special Publicity Department. Bussy was a maverick, as Smith recalled:

He was full of ideas, but like geniuses, he needed keeping down to earth. I had to sit on him pretty hard continually.

Bussy drew a 10% commission on his schemes, on top of a handsome salary of £1,000 a year. Newspapers frequently organised publicity stunts in bids to attract more readers, particularly those from the newly-affluent lower-middle classes. At a time of intense rivalry with the Daily Express, exhibitions were a useful form of publicity in addition to the more usual bill-posting and roadside hoarding. The first exhibition organised by the Special Publicity Department was the Daily Mail Exhibition of British and Irish Lace, on 9 March, 1908 at the Royal Horticultural Hall. The exhibition was designed to show the wide range of beautiful lace made at Home, as opposed to that of foreign manufacture. Articles in the Daily Mail reveal that a fear of French imports threatening the Irish and English lace industries was one of the reasons for the exhibition. The choice of lace as a subject may have been to link in with a tradition of the display of lace that went right back to the Great Exhibition. Lace was also

regarded as being a feminine interest and so would appeal to the female audience that Northcliffe wanted for the Daily Mail. The exhibition was very successful and attracted large crowds, but through some calculating moves a fast turnover of visitors was achieved:

On a very hot afternoon the place was overcrowded, and there was a queue waiting to go in. The people inside showed no disposition to hurry away. Bussy, ever resourceful, solved the difficulty by closing all the windows and doors. The people soon began to get headaches, and many felt faint (they were nearly all women), and in half an hour we had the hall clear and able to take in more people.

The Lace Exhibition generated £1,400 worth of advertising revenue, and sales of the Daily Mail in lace-making centres grew substantially. The success of the Lace Exhibition supported the Special Publicity Department's plans for a future Ideal Home Exhibition by showing that a large female audience existed for such events.

THE ARCHITECT'S MONOPOLY

Although Smith had by now successfully enticed drapers into advertising in the Daily Mail, he thought that their advertising would be limited by their capacity to supply any particular article, since demand might easily outstrip supply. He therefore sent Bussy to look for an industry 'with an almost inexhaustible capacity to supply any demand that could be created by advertising'. Bussy started with the building industry and discovered a highly interesting fact: firms depended for business on the recommendation of the architect. In return for a 15% commission on orders, architects recommended fittings and decorations to house purchasers. In his autobiography, Smith presented this state of affairs as restricting freedom of choice:

Their hold was so complete, in fact, that the home builder was left with no say whatever in the construction of his house, choice of fitting and decoration… Our task was clear. It was important to undermine the influence of the architect without delay, remove his stranglehold from the whole industry – 'clean up the racket', as my American friends would say. I was determined that the public should know the various and multitudinous things in existence which could make a house a home.

Above: A trip to the Ideal Home Exhibition was a special event, and visitors queued patiently to see inside the homes on display.

Above: From the early years, the show houses in the Village were always one of the most popular areas of the Ideal Home Exhibition. Even if visitors could not afford them, they offered a dream to aspire to.

With the exception of Aspinal's Enamel, which already advertised in the Daily Mail, retailers and manufacturers of paints, wallpapers, fire grates and other items connected with interior decoration advertised mainly in the trade press. How far Smith was instrumental in cutting out the architect's role as middle-man is difficult to ascertain, but he certainly had a considerable influence on patterns of shopping and consumption.

Smith realised he could not challenge the architects' business without offering something in return, so he devised a competition. A big prize would be offered for a design for an Ideal Home, surrounding the home with all the materials and gadgets that would contribute to its amenities and comfort. The title of the Ideal Home Exhibition was therefore designed to please architects, who also must have realised that their business would be stimulated by the publicity-grabbing exhibition medium.

THEMES BEHIND THE IDEAL HOME EXHIBITION

The Ideal Home Exhibition used the words 'the foundations of the nation's greatness are laid in the homes of the people' - a quote from HM King George V, taken from a speech he had made to the Convocation of York on 8 July 1910, to set a quasi-educational agenda. Although by 1908 manuals on domestic management were widely available, notably those by Mrs Peel, who sought to reassure those managing their homes with reduced domestic help, a visit to the Ideal Home Exhibition was a special event. People could actually see for themselves the latest gadgets and large goods that many shops did not have the room to display, while the Exhibition also educated them in the latest labour-saving ways and entertained them with fantastic spectacles, which presented home-making as both scientific and glamorous.

The Ideal Home Exhibition succeeded because it built on forms of entertainment that the public were already well accustomed to. Following the Great Exhibition in 1851, there was a series of high profile international exhibitions in London and other metropolitan centres and there were also many trade and commercial exhibitions that were part of the same culture of the spectacular. The Daily Mail announced that 1908 would be known as Exhibition Year, and listed 'twenty-five great shows', including the Franco-British Exhibition at White City and the Hungarian Exhibition at Earl's Court. The range of exhibitions on offer was extraordinary. It included the Heavy Motor Exhibition, the Sociological Society's Toy Exhibition, the Orient in London, Home Arts and Industries and the Brewers' Exhibition. What is startling is how few of these exhibitions are remembered, even though some of them were annual events and have very long histories. The success of exhibitions was dependent on both willing exhibitors and an enthusiastic public. In fact, the public were so keen on exhibitions that they often gatecrashed fairs which were not really intended for them. The Daily Mail advertised and reported on exhibitions of all kinds, whether they were intended for the public or not. This may partly have been for the benefit of readers employed as sales representatives in the appropriate trades.

Below and Overleaf: The show houses were built at speed, since there was often not much time available before the Exhibition opened. This often led to them being erected in record time – which the companies concerned were quick to use in their advertising.

Although the Ideal Home Exhibition had some similarities to trade or wholesale fairs, one of its main purposes was not only the display, but also the retail sale to the general public of novel and popular commodities. In addition, it not only showed all the latest domestic equipment, but also included entertaining and educational features about the lives of others around the world, particularly those from countries which were part of the British Empire.

At the beginning of the 1900s, Britain possessed the largest empire the world had ever seen. Over one quarter of the globe, some 12 million square miles, was coloured pink and Britain ruled a quarter of the world's population. The Ideal Home Exhibition showed a more domestic view of Empire than the international exhibitions and frequently featured anthropological displays, representing 'primitive' peoples not just as exotic others, but also as domesticated imperial subjects. In addition, the anthropological displays helped to instil a sense of stability in the face of intense anxieties about status and class in England. The glimpses of life overseas also encouraged so-called surplus women to emigrate to the colonies. Empire goods were also well represented at the Exhibition: between 1926 and 1933 the Empire Marketing Board organised displays that encouraged consumers to see the Empire as England's larder. Britain's relationship with the Empire allowed food and raw materials to be imported cheaply and the Imperial Preference system allowed Britain to give tariff protection to her own industry in home and Empire markets. In 1929, for example, the Empire supplied about one quarter of Britain's imports (by value), but Britain exported approximately 10% more to the Empire than was imported. 'Empire people' also formed an important market for home goods, especially medicines and teaching materials.

Looking at the displays of Ideal Homes, visitors to the Exhibition could fantasise that they lived the lives projected in them. They could believe that they, too, lived in an up-to-date Tudor home, or that their daughters had a charming little cottage like Princess Elizabeth for frolic time. They could become legitimate voyeurs, and visitors queued patiently to gain admittance to the houses. The absence of dividing walls gave them unobstructed views of, for example, dining room tables with sparkling cutlery glued to their surfaces. Stands also masqueraded as rooms, with manufacturers sponsoring every fitting. Souvenir postcards commemorated what they had seen and these could be posted to friends from the Exhibition with a special postmark. Some of the photographs have a very surreal quality, with perfect settings intruded upon by the lights hanging from Olympia's ceiling on long flexes. One photograph shows a workman fixing artificial blossom to a real tree which has been imported to Olympia and planted outside the mock Tudor village.

Lord Northcliffe was doubtful about the value of exhibitions to his newspaper as, like many of his time, he thought advertising was rather vulgar and ungentlemanly. His main concern was that the Ideal Home Exhibition would act as a promotional tool for the

Left: The Exhibition did a great deal to bring modern technology into the home, featuring new ideas – such as television – as they appeared and encouraging people to regard them as desirable.

Below Left: From the early days, children were considered an essential feature of the ideal home and were part of the Exhibition. Displays across the years showed different methods of childcare across the world, the latest furniture and equipment and even toys. In later years the Exhibition included a crèche, so that children could be left in safety while their parents visited other stands.

newspaper to attract new readers, rather than to raise advertising revenue. He refused to visit the first two Exhibitions in 1908 and 1910, but was finally persuaded by his wife to visit the third one in 1912. The enthusiasm of Smith and Bussy was therefore crucial to the survival of the Exhibition. In fact, they both also had good personal reason to support it, since they each received royalties of 5% of the net profits.

The Grand Hall (later renamed Olympia) in Hammersmith provided the venue for the Ideal Home Exhibition from 1908 until the 1980s. With 210,000 square feet of floor space, it was the largest building of its type in London. The appeal of the Exhibition was staggering in comparison with attendance at museums. For example, between 160,000 and 200,000 visitors attended the Exhibition in 1908 during the 14 days it was open. In comparison, the British Museum attracted 754,872 people in 1912 over the whole year (which was a rise of 31,000 on the previous year). The tenth Ideal Home Exhibition in 1926 was seen by 497,336 people, by 1937 attendance had climbed to 620,000 and it reached an all-time high of 1,329,644 in 1957.

BETWEEN THE WARS

During the First World War, the exhibition activities of the Special Publicity Department temporarily ceased, but by 1918, Smith and Bussy were planning to revive the Ideal Home Exhibition. The same year, Odhams, the publisher, set up Ideal Home magazine, which incensed Northcliffe and fuelled his doubts as to whether the Exhibition should continue. There was nothing he could do to prevent them using the title and he was alarmed by the thought that the Ideal Home Exhibition could be seen as publicising the magazine, rather than the Daily Mail.

When the first post-war Ideal Home Exhibition was held in 1920, Northcliffe was still furious about Odhams' magazine. He declared in his daily communiqué to Daily Mail staff that they should ensure that the Ideal Home Exhibition was inextricably linked with the Daily Mail, and even suggested that the name of the exhibition should be changed to The Daily Mail Exhibition. Bussy reassured him that the primary purpose of the Exhibition was to advertise the Daily Mail, but also pointed out that it made a great deal of money. He suggested that these profits should not become part of the company's general profits, but should be used to start a propaganda fund with which to meet competition. The usual way to stave off competition was through advertising and by the staging of special promotions, which often cost a good deal of money to finance. The Ideal Home Exhibition would thus perform a double function, acting both as a form of publicity and as a means of generating income to finance other 'puffs'.

Despite Northcliffe's complaints, Bussy was soon busy organising another Ideal Home Exhibition in 1922. His main concern was still the potential of the Ideal Home to generate extra advertising revenue for the Daily Mail, but he also sought to calm Northcliffe's fears by claiming that of the over a quarter of a million people who had paid for admission at the turnstiles, he had not heard of one who had been disappointed.

ONE OF A KIND

The Ideal Home Exhibition was the first exhibition of its kind in the world and has been much imitated. The most notable imitation is the French Salon des Art Ménagers, which was held between 1923 and 1976. This exhibition originated from a competition held for manufacturers of household appliances. Its initial emphasis was on technology and it had some striking similarities to the 1921 Daily Mail Efficiency Exhibition. The Salon des Art Ménagers later expanded to include products related to the equipment, furniture and decoration of the home, as well as domestic appliances. The Ideal Home Exhibition still has its imitators: in 1980 there were 41 exhibitions that used the words 'Ideal Home' in their title in the United Kingdom, plus another 5 overseas.

The Ideal Home Exhibition has told a different history of the domestic interior to that of the tasteful galleries of decorative arts museums. It has presented a design history that largely rejected the Arts and Crafts movement and Modernism, but still embraced modernity. The Exhibition has addressed women explicitly as consumers, while museums often assume a 'neutral' viewer. Museums also tend to collect objects for their own sake, ignoring their context and social significance, while their presentation of objects often gives a false impression of their availability, affordability and use.

Many of the gadgets sold at the Ideal Home Exhibition are not the tasteful classics of the design museums; instead they tend to be ephemeral and cheap. However, they also often seem to be highly valued by their owners, who would not spare them for the 1991 Ideal Homes exhibition at the Design Museum because they were too useful.

Despite, or perhaps because of, its undoubted appeal, cultural commentators have often dismissed the Ideal Home Exhibition. Many have felt uncomfortable with its reflection of consumer aspirations for goods and lifestyles that they have thought of as frivolous and empty. Yet the history of the Ideal Home Exhibition is the history of the hopes, dreams and aspirations of the respectable working classes and middle classes, of conservative and ordinary people.

Opposite: Princess Elizabeth looking round the Berg House in 1949. From the beginning there was a tradition of Royal involvement with the Ideal Home Exhibition. This ranged from actually participating – such as the Queen exhibiting items from The Royal Technical Schools at Sandringham at the first Exhibition in 1908 - to perhaps performing the opening ceremony, or merely paying a private visit.

Overleaf: The Village often featured a variety of house styles next door to one another. The effect was made even more surreal by the pendant lights and normal exhibition stands around them.

CHAPTER ONE

'Home Sweet Home'
The First Exhibitions

At the turn of the century, when the Daily Mail Ideal Home Exhibition was founded, there was a real sense of living in a new world that had broken with the past as never before. As well as social and cultural changes, the explosion of scientific knowledge and the development of technology led to different production methods that resulted in new forms of work. In pursuit of this new work, people moved from rural to urban centres and, consequently, cities grew enormously. Developments in transport and communications made movement both within cities and around the Empire much easier. Better educational opportunities and the spread of literacy also expanded the horizons of work for many people. There were new work opportunities in government departments as a result of increased state intervention and regulation, and more clerical and managerial work with the emergence of big business. The real improvement, although small, in the living standards of most people meant that they now had some surplus money to spend and extra leisure time available. The Daily Mail and its Ideal Home Exhibition appealed to the aspirations of these people now moving up the social ladder.

Above: A bungalow built for the 1908 Exhibition by Bridge Barrett and furnished by Thomas Wallis & Co. The Tudor style remained popular and was often featured in buildings for the Exhibition.

THE FIRST IDEAL HOME EXHIBITION

On Friday, 9 October, 1908 the first Daily Mail Ideal Home Exhibition was opened at Olympia by the Lord Mayor of London, Sir John Bell. The band of the 1st Life Guards played the opening bars of John Howard Payne's 'Home Sweet Home'. The words of this popular American song, which was often found in cross-stitch embroideries on parlour walls, were also featured on the frontispiece of the 6d guide to the Exhibition.

Encouraged by the roaring success of the Daily Mail Lace Exhibition earlier in the year, Smith and Bussy announced that the Ideal Home Exhibition:

will be unique not only in its interest, but in the huge field it will cover. There are upwards of twelve sections, each dealing with a separate phase of home life, and each comprising an exhibition in itself. This means that all that is best in twelve ordinary exhibitions will be condensed into the Ideal Home Exhibition.

The timing meant that the Ideal Home Exhibition ran on the tail end of the Franco-British Exhibition, which had closed after a run of five months at White City. Smith and Bussy no doubt hoped to attract some of the millions of people who had visited the Franco-British Exhibition. The timing was certainly effective; by the time the Ideal Home Exhibition closed on Saturday, 24 October, it had attracted some 160,000 visitors. Although the scale of the Ideal Home Exhibition paled into insignificance alongside the Franco-British Exhibition, and many of its component themes had been seen before at international exhibitions and trade fairs, what made the Ideal Home Exhibition unique was its sole emphasis on the home. The publicity for the forthcoming exhibition pointed out that only a few had the gift to create an 'ideal home' unaided, and that most people relied upon suggestions and advice from others. The Exhibition was offered as a kind of three-dimensional advice manual.

Daily Mail.

Daily Circulation Five Times as Large as That of Any Penny London Morning Journal.

WEDNESDAY, MARCH 25, 1908.   LONDON.   MANCHESTER.   PARIS.   NO. 3,729.   ONE HALFPENNY.

"An Englishman's Home is his Castle"

The
Ideal Home
Exhibition

Organised and Promoted by the

Daily Mail.

Olympia, London, W.

Friday, October 9th, to Saturday, October 24th, 1908.

TO display—in a manner and on a scale that has never been attempted before—all that will conduce to the comfort, convenience, entertainment, health and well being of home life will be the purpose of this Exhibition. It will diffuse a knowledge of the most improved implements and contrivances of inventive science and all else that will tend to the enrichment and easing of life, or the beauty and charm of home. To express the highest attainment in utility, art or science—in a word, "The Ideal Home"—is its object.

SECTIONS :

CONSTRUCTION,	RECREATION,
DECORATION,	HYGIENE AND
LIGHTING AND	CLEANING,
HEATING,	FOOD AND
SANITATION,	COOKERY,
VENTILATION,	GARDEN AND
FURNITURE,	ACCESSORIES.

As the scope of the Exhibition is so wide it will only be possible to allot space in each section to those who will undertake to arrange the most interesting exhibits. For further particulars apply,

Special Publicity Dept.,
"Daily Mail" Offices,
3, Tallis St., London, E.C.

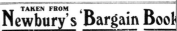

The Daily Mail described the main features of the stalls and exhibits as: how to build a home; how to equip a home; the baby in the home; the garden; home work. The exhibition brought together a wide range of manufacturers and retailers, most concerned with mass-produced goods from the new industries that the Daily Mail wanted to target as advertisers in the newspapers. Unfortunately, no plan exists for the first Exhibition, but the Daily Mail described it as:

a little town with thirteen long thoroughfares, lined with houses and stalls. Some of the houses are substantial-looking structures, two storeys high, and every form of art is represented.

The plans and designs entered by nearly 450 architects for the Architects' Competition were displayed in the Gallery. The competition was for cottages in three price bands, with a Gold, Silver and Bronze medal being awarded in each category, and the competition judge was Sir Edwin Lutyens. A further competition was open to visitors to the Exhibition, in which they selected their Ideal Home from the architects' plans, and then proceeded to furnish it entirely from items displayed at the Exhibition. There was also an Arts & Crafts competition, entered by people from all around the world, covering every section of arts and crafts from painting to poker work, book binding to wood carving.

Several aristocratic women were involved in the Exhibition, including the Queen, who exhibited items from The Royal Technical Schools at Sandringham. The Times (also owned by Northcliffe) thus gave the Exhibition advance notice in its 'Court Circular' column. The presence of the 'ladies' gave the Exhibition a sense of glamour, although it was mainly designed to appeal to home-makers, which were naturally assumed to be women.

One of the main sections was Hygiene and Cleaning. The 1904 Interdepartmental Committee on Physical Deterioration criticised working-class housewives for their domestic incompetence, despite evidence from their own witnesses suggesting that this was due to poverty and poor housing. Rather than actually supplying material improvements, such as

Above: Overall view of the 1908 Exhibition from the western end of the gallery. Several still well-known names can be seen - including chocolate makers J.S. Fry & Sons and Bird's Custard. The Millennium stand in the foreground featured an 'Ideal Loaf' competition, which was judged by visitors to the stand.

Opposite: The first advertisement for the very first Ideal Home Exhibition, on the front page of the Daily Mail dated March 26, 1908.

THE IDEAL HOME.

Above: Sketch and photograph of the Ideal Home that formed the centrepiece of the 1910 Exhibition, designed by Mr Rupert Davison. The house had a living room, parlour, four bedrooms, a bathroom and a kitchen and could be built at the time for just £600, with the furnishings for the entire house costing an additional £350.

sanitation and hot water, medical officers tried to educate women in the art of mothering in order to improve infant mortality both at home in Britain and in the colonies. Emphasis was placed on hygiene, with the burden of cleanliness being placed on women. The Hygiene and Cleaning section reflected this obsession with cleanliness. The section offered both mistress and servant ways of 'banishing the devil of darkness and disease', for example with a vacuum cleaning system and a system of clothes washing without soap; the latest technology was used to fight the war against germs.

BABYLAND

The second Boer War (1889-1902) had also highlighted the considerable numbers of children who did not survive infancy and the poor physical condition of those who did, with many urban working-class men being rejected for active service. There were also fears about a population decline due not only to the high infant mortality rate, but also to a falling birth rate among the middle classes. Therefore another major section was Babyland, which offered advice on the care of children and demonstrated 'what is being done to diminish the deplorable infant mortality which is a blot on the country'. Twelve babies were put on display: 'probably the youngest subjects of the King who have ever earned a weekly wage - the parents will be paid 10s a week'.

The National Association of Day Nurseries showed a crèche staffed by trained nurses - 'in which children will be tended just as they are in the slum districts where such institutions exist' - for the children of poor mothers who had no choice but to go out to work. However, it was unlikely that the poorer mothers who were most in need of help could have afforded to visit the exhibition.

Great Ormond Street Hospital for Children put a specimen ward and crèche on display to illustrate the treatment of infantile complaints, the main attraction of which was an incubator. The display addressed the fears of middle-class women for the health of their children, who were still struck down by childhood diseases such as whooping cough and pneumonia, despite their higher standards of hygiene, improved medical services, smaller families and better incomes. Two Ward Sisters were on hand to give advice to visitors, among whom were assumed to be large numbers of nurses (who were typical Daily Mail readers) - so much so that a special rendezvous was arranged for them.

In the first decade of the twentieth century there were also anxieties about the

decline of traditional rural industries in both England and overseas. The Exhibition therefore featured a display of 'Home Industries' that included Indian embroidery exhibited by Lady Victoria Carbery, and an Indian woman weaving a carpet. Lady Carbery suggested that the various Home Industries Societies could provide suitable work for the 'thousands of our country people' who crowd to the towns and add to the ranks of casual labourers. She also advised the public to buy the good quality work of home industries, such as that displayed at the Exhibition, in preference to cheap, imported goods. The proceeds from her Ideal Home Exhibition stand were to be used to build a home for white working women and girls in Simla for whom the riches promised by emigration had failed to materialise.

On the first day of the Exhibition, an article reviewing the exhibits appeared in the

Above: View down the main street of the Dutch Village, created by the Netherlands Chamber of Commerce at the 1912 Exhibition. On the right is the Town Hall, a copy of the town hall at Woerden, and at the end of the street is a village inn selling aromatic Dutch liqueurs.

Daily Mail, surrounded by advertisements for the companies and products it claimed to review. The text of the article was remarkably similar to the text of the adverts, and in fact it was what today would be called an advertisement feature or an advertorial. It was notable that the advertisers worked the word 'ideal' into their copy at every opportunity. Initially, advertisements appeared only in the Daily Mail, and not in the Exhibition catalogue itself until 1913.

Much of the coverage in the Daily Mail for the next Ideal Home Exhibition in 1910 concerned the needs of brides or newly-weds, and the paper declared that the Exhibition had been organised:

with the idea principally of assisting married folk and their families. It has been felt that no home can be really ideal unless it contains at least one man, one woman, and, if possible, one baby, or else a good substitute.

The Daily Mail also declared that the Exhibition offered practical help to everyone with a home, and advised visitors to prepare for their trip in advance by looking round their homes carefully for any obstacles to its smooth running that they wished to get out of the way.

THE TUDOR VILLAGE

One of the main features of the 1910 Exhibition was a Tudor Village, which presented an idyllic version of 'Merrie England' and offered an 'atmosphere of old-time peace and quiet':

A number of quaint, half-timbered cottages are grouped about a village green, amid beds of gaily-coloured flowers and beneath the green leaves of stout old trees. This is one of the most picturesque features of the Exhibition. It is believed that such an elaborate exhibit has never before been arranged for an exhibition of such duration. Visitors will find it a most delightful spot, both for its beauty and interest, and as a place to rest on the benches round the village inn, under the trees, or near the foaming waterfall.

Firms that had been in continuous business for at least a hundred years occupied the buildings, which were staffed by people in Tudor dress. The village included a barber's shop (manned by Messrs. A & F Pears, manufacturers of soap), an old tea store, Italian warehouse, loom, fire station, and an inn 'with mine host and buxom barmaid' dispensing 'various old-time beverages'. The application for a licence to serve alcohol in the inn was unfortunately turned down: the judge on the case declared that the 'pretence village' would have to have 'pretence drinking'. A maypole, ducking stool and stocks added to the supposed historical accuracy of the village. Real grass covered the asphalt floor of the Olympia annexe, together with 'old-fashioned' plants, shrubs and garden ornaments.

For all its supposedly accurate historical detail, the Tudor Village was a fantasy, a place of dreams and desires. It was a theatre in which visitors could themselves become players. They were invited to travel through time and space and were then able to send a postcard of their historical journey. One such postcard showed a group of costumed drinkers outside the village inn as if it were a snapshot of Tudor life. In most of the others, however, the illusion was shattered; glimpses of the girders supporting Olympia's ceiling could be seen, as well as the suspended lighting.

During this period, the ideal was to live in a mock-Tudor or 'Tudorbethan' semi-detached house and these were the most characteristic form of housing in the Ideal Home Exhibition between 1908 and 1939. The Tudorbethan houses on show in the interwar years were not wattle and daub reconstructions of the past, but constructed out of the most up-to-date materials, furnished with Jacobethan reproduction furniture mass-produced by the latest techniques and containing the most modern kitchen and bathroom fittings available. The Tudorbethan style evoked a majestic past, far removed from the reality of England's diminishing world status and declining Empire. It was also a specifically English style, as against the foreign classicism of Greek and Roman architecture. Tudorbethan made reference to many historical styles, using bays, porches, gables and dormers to break up the overall building mass. The unplanned individuality of the Tudorbethan house contrasted strongly with the plain neo-Georgian architecture of local authority housing estates. Semi-detached Tudorbethan houses were laid out in pairs of alternating design, emphasising their individuality and difference from one another; neo-Georgian houses were planned in a collective, unifying style to enhance the similarities of houses in a scheme. Tudorbethan was, then, emphatically different from council housing and so appealed to people's aspirations.

Above: Commemorative postcard showing the Tudor Village that was created in the Annexe for the 1910 Exhibition.

Below: The buildings of the Tudor Village were occupied by firms that had been in business for at least 100 years. Many of the names are still in business today - such as Crosse & Blackwell, Heal & Son, Twining & Co., Schweppes Ltd and A.F Pears.

Right: The Tudor Village was complete with village green and a pond. The ducking stool was provided for the punishment of 'nagging wives and witches', and there was also a set of stocks for holding 'in a vice-like grip, the limbs of some sturdy vagabond'.

THE VIROL NURSERY

In the 1910 Babyland section, the National Society of Day Nurseries crèche appeared again, as well as a second 'oriental'-style nursery, The Nursery of All Nations, that was filled with children of every race to form a cosmopolitan colony. The 'black, brown, yellow and white' babies were 'lent' by judges, barristers and government officials, as well as 'those who are glad to accept the help of the charities which look after their offspring'. This display also featured 'native nurses'. All the babies were to be treated alike, and medically examined every day. 'Babies of All Nations' was sponsored by the manufacturers of Virol, a proprietary mixture used to build up infants to ward against infections that was taken by bottle-fed babies in their milk and by older children with their meals.

Virol issued a series of postcards featuring some of the children to commemorate the Ideal Home Exhibition display. The postcards show individual photographs of children, identified by their name and country of origin, posed against a studio backdrop in supposedly national costume. The authenticity of the models is open to question; the same hat and string of beads appears in several of the photographs on different children. Despite this, the photographs had an appealing directness in their fairly informal poses, which echoed those found in English family albums, and their effect may have been to stress the similarity of children, rather than their differences. The geographical separation of the English babies from the others, however, invited visitors to make comparisons and contrasts. The Nursery of All Nations illustrated baby life and customs: 'how the little ones laugh and cry and play'. By contrast, the dozen English babies would be 'all no doubt on their best behaviour and setting a good example to their foreign visitors'!

THE 1912 EXHIBITION

In the build-up to the 1912 Ideal Home Exhibition, the Daily Mail declared that 'all the world and her husband flocked to the last two Ideal Home Exhibitions, and will do so again next month'. However, despite the fact that there was an attempt to make the Exhibitions held before the First World War appeal to all classes of the community, the entrance fee of 6d would have been beyond the reach of most members of the working class. The range of new products and appliances on view could certainly make housework easier and more pleasant, but only if one could afford them. However, even those who could only afford the entrance fee were offered a fantasy of domestic life into which they could project themselves. The

Exhibition was also offered as an object lesson to domestic servants.

The winning design of the Ideal Home competition in 1912 was an eleven-roomed, half-timbered, detached house that was later built in the Kent suburb of Park Langley, Beckenham, and offered for sale at £1,100. There were over 700 plans submitted for the competition and, although two of the judges were architects, there were also two ladies 'possessed of a considerable knowledge of practical domestic architecture', chosen by the Daily Mail to represent the views of 'ordinary' suburban housewives.

The Exhibition maintained a careful balance of old and new, showing both well-tried items and modern appliances and gadgets. One woman visitor said:

…there are so many things here that you do want, or would want if you dared to, that you must have some of them one day, if not all of them at once.

Left: Illustration from the 1912 catalogue of the Ideal House, which won first prize in the Daily Mail Ideal Homes competition. It was designed by Mr Reginald Fry and built as the centrepiece of the 1912 Ideal Home Exhibition by H.G. Taylor, of Park Langley in Kent.

Below: The house was built for real at Park Langley, and cost £1,100 including fittings such as stoves. This photograph shows it early in 1972.

Above: Detail from an advertisement for Broadwood pianos in the 1913 Exhibition catalogue. Their stand not only displayed their latest models, but also featured a collection of rare instruments illustrating the history of the piano from the clavichord onwards. This included the player-piano which had accompanied the Scott expedition to the South Pole.

Above and right: Two of the postcards issued by Virol to commemorate their display at the 1912 Exhibition. Babies of All Nations contained a small representative of each country where Virol was trading, and the postcards showed them in what was supposed to be their national costume. Virol was recommended in cases of malnutrition and consumption and in all cases where the child - or adult - required building up.

HOME-MAKING AND LABOUR-SAVING

As well as instructing women in the joys of consumption, the Ideal Home Exhibition was seen as a tool with which young women could be educated in the skills of home-making. Mothers were advised to take their daughters 'to show them what can be done and is done in the housekeeping world today' and schoolmistresses were urged to do likewise with their female charges. Labour-saving tools were presented as a way of making traditional housewifely duties easier 'with a saving of temper and physical fatigue', rather than as a radical way of freeing women to allow them to pursue new interests or careers. The feminine skills of housekeeping and child-rearing were thought too important to be left to experience, but ought instead to be learned through instruction. Thus information was offered in the form of lectures and demonstrations in subjects such as bee-keeping and jam-making.

The 1912 Exhibition was also offered as a kind of moral training course, presenting marriage as knowledgeable consumption and dutiful motherhood and producing respectable couples. One journalist in the Daily Mail described the adventures of Colin and Barbara, the 'ideal couple', at Olympia. At the beginning of their visit they were not engaged; Colin thought matrimony 'a stuffy, dullish institution, which necessitated the tedious process of taking a flat or house and filling it with uninspiring chairs and monotonous tables'. Barbara, however, dazzled Colin with an 'unexpected display of housewifely knowledge', grasping the scientific principles of an advanced curtain rod design and proving to Colin that there was more to her than the 'chafing, sporting, slangy little friend' that he knew. Overwhelmed, too, by Barbara's display of tenderness at 'Babyland', a vision came to Colin as they toured the Ideal House that revealed to him the 'Ideal Life'. On the tube home he proposed to Barbara, asking her to 'live in a house like that'. A visit to the Ideal Home Exhibition could, then, even result in matrimony!

Babyland featured an even more spectacular Virol nursery in 1912, built in the style of an Indian house and containing over 100 babies of all nationalities. Marble steps led down from the house into an enclosed courtyard with a fountain, flowers and birds. Perhaps there had been criticisms of the nursery the previous year; the Daily Mail declared that this year it was to be a children's party, not a baby show: 'the adult visitors... are to be permitted to look on from outside the enclosing barriers, but not to look at anything in the nature of a

performance'. The children lived in three large specially-furnished houses in Kensington, under the supervision of a doctor and nurses. The Daily Mail assured its readers that the babies would have 'complete quietude and privacy' and that visitors 'will only have the opportunity of looking on at their happiness during the daily periods when they are taken out to play in their Indian garden'.

ART FURNITURE

Avant-garde ideas about design were first included in the Ideal Home Exhibition in 1913, in an Art Furniture section. Influenced by the Arts and Crafts movement, art furnishing reacted against early ornate Victorian style in favour of plainer and simpler furnishings and more informal arrangements of rooms. Furniture that disguised the way it was made, or the materials it was made of, was particularly discouraged. The section contained English, Belgian, Dutch and French rooms, most of which were unexceptional, although the Belgian room contained a hint of Art Nouveau in its wallpapers: 'rich in strange colours, complex but concise in design'.

The most daring room was that designed by the Omega Workshops. Omega was a commercial decorative arts group, connected to the Bloomsbury Group and supported by liberal and wealthy patrons. The Omega sitting room was called a Post-Impressionist room in the Daily Mail:

The wall panels surrounded by plain rectangular surfaces of blue, strawboard colour, and dark chocolate, represent - if so crude a word may be used for an art that tries to avoid the representation of anything approaching reality - dancing figures, or rather, the abstract rhythm and volume of dancing figures, expressed in systems of spheric intersecting curves tinted in rose-colour and light green.

The painted designs on the furniture and walls were reminiscent of avant-garde European artists such as Cézanne and Picasso. The clean lines and stark simplicity of the furniture were influenced by the Arts and Crafts movement. Marquetry was of distinctly cubist character and the carpet was geometrically patterned in daring, though tastefully contrasted, colours.

The Daily Mail's main motive in including the Omega room was perhaps to provoke some of the criticism and notoriety that an exhibition of Post-Impressionism had received three years earlier. Certainly the newspaper reports of it concentrated on its shock value and many visitors disliked it on sight. It also led to a major split within the Omega group, less than six months after it had been set up.

Above: The Moore & Moore stand from the 1910 Exhibition. Moore & Moore produced inexpensive player-pianos and pianos that were entirely made in Britain.

Left: An early Hovis stand, promoting Hovis (Strength of Man) bread as a nourishing food – the company claimed it had 'flesh-forming and bone-making properties'. Hovis were in fact only the millers and the bread was baked by local bakers using their flour.

Above: The Schoolhouse from the Russian Village at the 1913 Exhibition. The village featured exact replicas of rural Russian buildings and occupied the entire two acres of the Annexe.

Above Right: A North Russian log house. The village was arranged with the co-operation of Countess Sheremetiev, President of the Kustarny Organisation of St Petersburg. 'Kustarny' were Russian peasant handicrafts and examples were displayed in each house in the village.

By contrast, another art furniture display at the 1913 Ideal Home Exhibition received a rapturous reception, generating numerous approving column inches: the rooms of Mr H.K. Prosser. These were a 'Moonlight Sonata' music room, a Watteau room, a day nursery and a night nursery. The Beethoven room interpreted its theme by using a blue and silver colour scheme throughout, which extended even to the silver piano. The Watteau room contained an original painting by the artist and, to focus attention on this, a chimney piece was designed in the shape of a bank of golden clouds with a central sun flanked by two smaller ones containing concealed electric lights whose rays were concentrated on the picture. The day nursery had a nautical theme and the night nursery was covered with silver stars. The idea of art furniture was thus interpreted here as escapist fantasy and illusionism, rather than Modernist simplicity.

HOMES FROM OTHER LANDS

The Ideal Home Exhibition often displayed homes from earlier periods and foreign cultures alongside present day ones to show just how far the modern English home had evolved. In 1910, for example, Derry and Toms, the famous Kensington High Street store, erected a 'wonderful fifteenth century cottage' brought over from Russia. The brightly-painted and carved surface of the cottage was contrasted with a model modern dining room. The Daily Mail commented:

from the heart of Russia to London, and from the fifteenth to the twentieth century, is a journey not often condensed within ten paces and made in a moment.

In the 1912 Exhibition a 'typical Dutch village with inhabitants in national costume' was featured. There was a village street with a town hall, doctor's house and parsonage. Nearby was a burgomaster's house, as well as two working windmills. A row of shops included craftsmen at work, while girls in national costume sold national produce. A reproduction of a Frisian farm showed Dutch cheeses being made. The wooden houses each had their own garden with trees 'cut in the quaint Dutch fashion'. A tulip field containing fifty thousand flowers - with canals running through it and bordered by willows - faded into a painting of a typical Dutch landscape at the horizon. The village had royal patronage; the Queen of Holland gave her approval and the Dutch Queen Mother sent 50,000 artificial flowers to be sold for charity.

In 1913 an 'exact replica of a typical Russian village' could be visited at the Exhibition. The village displayed peasant arts and handicrafts, with the support of the Russian government. Following the success of the display, Derry and Toms held a Russian Fair after the Exhibition closed, which suggests that Russian design had an aura of fashionability at the time.

After its successful beginnings, the Exhibition had to be postponed for six years because of the First World War and only returned in 1920.

CHAPTER TWO

Homes fit for Heroes

The Twenties

LABOUR-SAVING HOUSE.

Third Prize. Entrance Front.

After a gap of seven years, the first Ideal Home Exhibition after the First World War was held in 1920. One of the 'puffs' to mark the re-emergence of the Exhibition was a competition for Ideal (Workers') Homes. The theme of the competition could not have been more topical and popular, since the Housing Act of 1919 had promised 'homes fit for heroes' to reward soldiers, munitions workers and their families, who lived in appalling conditions. The entries had to follow the latest recommendations and standards and were based around two types of plan for industrial areas and two for rural areas, which were designed to be practical and labour-saving. Although the plans were fixed, the style of architecture and the materials were not, which allowed architects to use regional styles as appropriate. The prizes panel of seven judges included three architects, a social reformer, a representative from the Women's Co-Operative Guild and the chairman of the Garden Cities and Town Planning Association. This was unusual, in that competitions were usually judged only by technical experts. In addition, a committee of working men's wives in each area adjudicated on any departures from the standards laid down.

The country was divided into four areas, and books of the best of the 3,500 plans entered for the competition, with the names and addresses of the architects, were published as a service to local councils. Prizes were awarded in only three categories, since none of the designs for the Welsh industrial area were thought to be suitable. The winning designs were built to a height of 4ft. 6ins. only, to enable them to be looked into as well as walked through.

LABOUR-SAVING IDEAS AT THE EXHIBITION

Despite the Ideal (Workers') Homes competition being open only to architects, many of the women who were to live in the new houses wrote to the Daily Mail with suggestions.

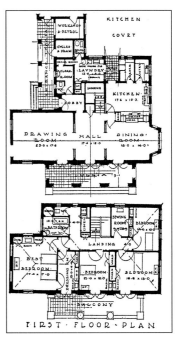

Above: Sketch and plans for the design that won third prize in the Labour-Saving House Exhibition. It was based on the premise that one person only would be managing the domestic duties and, unlike the designs which won first and second prizes, did not include a maid's room.

Left: The winning design for the Midland area in the Daily Mail Ideal (Workers') Homes competition.

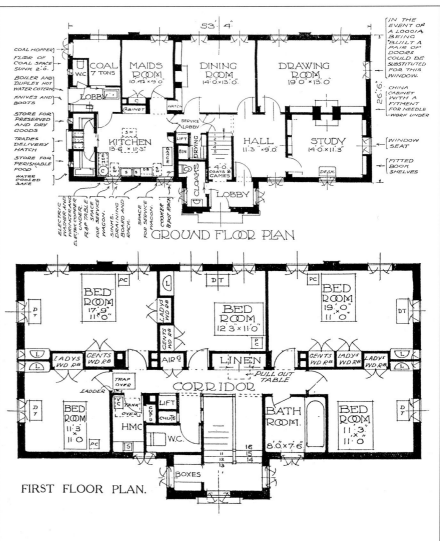

GROUND FLOOR PLAN

FIRST FLOOR PLAN.

Above Top & Right: Plans and sketch for the design that won first prize in the Labour-Saving House Exhibition. One of its ingenious features was the trades delivery hatch, which had self-locking compartments to receive packages and slate panels on the doors for messages to tradesmen, so eliminating the need to run to the back door every time a delivery van called.

Above: The Vickers cottage after 6 days construction. The entire cottage was built, complete with all its fixtures and fittings, in only ten days.

They asked for 'light and airy' houses and houses with 'attractive exteriors', but their strongest plea was said to be for labour-saving devices. In 1920 the Daily Mail therefore also held a competition for an Ideal Labour-Saving Home.

The competition offered three prizes, totalling £400, for the best design for a labour-saving house. It was pointed out that although such a house might cost more in the first place, it would be more economical to run and would also save labour. The winning design contained intrinsic labour-saving design features - not just domestic appliances - to reduce both housework and maintenance. Labour-saving features were focused on the kitchen, with the various appliances being grouped to minimise work in the preparation, cooking and serving of food and in washing and house-cleaning. The heights of the cooker, table, sinks and other worktops were scientifically determined at the most suitable level for a woman of average height. Rounded corners eliminated dust, mouldings were kept to a minimum, floors were damp-proof, all surfaces were easily cleaned, bright metal fittings were eliminated and windows could be cleaned from the inside. The house was heated by radiators run from a coal fire in the back lobby, and heating and cooking appliances were vitreous enamelled. These features, it was claimed, also aided hygiene.

The essential parts of the winning design were built and displayed at the Ideal Home Exhibition, along with a scale model of the complete house in neo-Georgian style. The house would have been too expensive for many Daily Mail readers, since it included five bedrooms, a fitted bathroom, central heating, hot and cold running water and electricity. It was aimed

particularly at the new salaried professionals, whom the Daily Mail sought to woo from the Express. It would also have appealed, above all, to readers' aspirations. It was intended to be run with domestic help; the plan shows a maid's room adjoining the kitchen.

The Daily Mail also solicited women's expert opinions on labour-saving ideas through other competitions. In 1920 the Daily Mail awarded prizes to its readers for 'the best individual labour-saving suggestions that could be compressed on a postcard'. T.H Windibank's design, one of the most ingenious commended entries, showed a labour-saving kitchen with a dresser that could also be accessed in the dining room, with a slate-lined safe underneath to store food. Windibank's dual-access dresser design meant that only one journey was needed from the kitchen to the dining room, instead of ten. Another of the commended designs was for an 'artisan scullery', which was the adaptation of 'the usual type of scullery sink' by the addition of a shelf to hold a washing bowl and a draining board. Above the sink was a draining rack for plates, beside it was a shelf to hold plates and beside that a pot stand, thus ensuring that everything was in easy reach.

Above: Overall view of the Township of Ideal Homes at the 1924 Exhibition. The modern houses on view ranged from a bungalow at £166 to a manor house at £2,500. In total there were thirteen houses, in as many different styles.

Above: An early 'dishwasher' at the 1920 Exhibition. The plates and dishes were loaded into the rack, and hot water was sprayed over them at pressure via a rubber pipe from the domestic supply.

Above Right: Listening to a portable wireless at the 1922 Exhibition. This set was advertised as being able to 'receive messages from as far distant as Paris and Poldhu without the use of an aerial'.

Right: 'Electricity's aids to the tea-table' - a photograph from the Daily Mail in 1920. Electrical appliances were still such a novelty that each item was labelled.

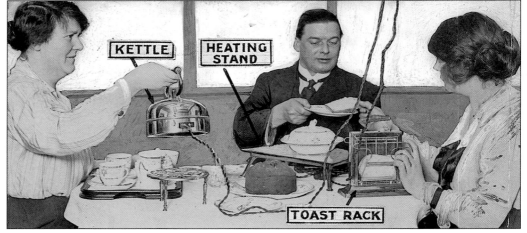

A group of housewives and designers who made up the Household Appliances Committee of the Design and Industries Association (DIA) judged the competition. The DIA had been founded in 1915 to improve design in British industry. The DIA strongly recommended simple, cheap, painted furniture, devoid of superfluous decoration. The furniture seemed modern and, indeed, shocking, to the public of the Ideal Home Exhibition. Wealth and social status were more clearly signified by decoration, and such furniture may also have had undesirable connotations of 'making-do'. Ironically, such designs were influenced by the Arts and Crafts movement, which drew on historical traditions, so what was thought of as modern looked both backwards and forwards. The messages of the DIA were promoted within the Ideal Home Exhibition not only as lessons in good design, but also warnings on bad design. The DIA contributed a domestic 'Chamber of Horrors' to the 1920 Exhibition, warning visitors what to avoid, in order to emphasise its message. The DIA

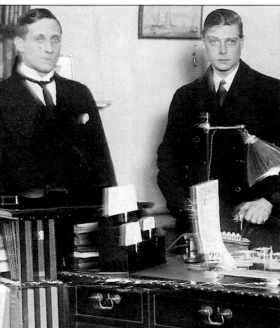

The Daily Mail exhibitions were regularly patronised by royalty. The top two photos show, left, King George V and the Queen at the 1921 Efficiency Exhibition and, right, the Duke of York (later King George VI) at the same exhibition. The bottom left picture is of the Prince of Wales (later Edward VIII) at the Efficiency Exhibition, while that at bottom right is the Duchess of York (now the Queen Mother) at the opening of the 1924 Ideal Home Exhibition.

demonstrated 'fitness for purpose' by showing the 'approved pattern' and the 'horrible example' in pairs. The DIA's sense of morality spilled over into the language that was used to describe the exhibit:

There is a depraved china milk-jug, for instance, with a hollow handle which fills with milk. The handle can never be properly cleaned and acts as a poison centre. A virtuous, sensible milk-jug will keep it company.

Labour-saving in general was part of a concern with the achievement of national efficiency, but was also a response to the servant problem after the First World War and the circumstances of the New Poor. The Labour-saving section, which had first been introduced in 1913, was one of the most popular sections in the Exhibition. It presented labour-saving appliances as a response to the servant problem. Many working-class women had been drafted into war work in factories, enabling them to give up the much-loathed domestic

service. They preferred the freedom and conditions of factory work and it paid better wages than domestic service, enabling them to purchase goods to ease their own domestic labour. Although many women were demobilised and forced back into domestic service after the war, there was still a shortage of good servants and the rise in working-class wages meant that they commanded higher salaries.

There were also the New Poor, who were trying to keep up the appearance of living in middle-class comfort, while actually living in penury. The New Poor were created by post-war inflation - their salaries had failed to keep up with the rise in prices, while the increases in taxation introduced during the war remained in force. The Daily Mail claimed they were a growing group. The concept was a brilliant strategy to appeal to the aspirations of the Daily Mail's readers, as it was to some extent self-defining; it allowed them to re-invent grander histories for themselves, to imagine themselves as people who had once had money but had now fallen on hard times. Although some members of the New Poor had never been able to afford the kind of lifestyle evoked, many did now have to cope with fewer servants, and they also began to move to smaller homes.

HOUSEWORK AND HOME-MAKING

By 1920, women's lives in particular had changed in enormous ways. During the First World War, many middle-class women had gained a sense of independence by working as nurses or doing voluntary work. The granting of suffrage in 1917 to those over 30 who were householders, or the wife of a householder, gave women legal and political rights as citizens. The role of the housewife was constantly redefined - she could be chancellor of the domestic economy, skilled personnel manager of truculent and lazy servants or professional home economist using the latest American scientific management techniques and labour-saving devices in her laboratory-kitchen. The home-making features in the women's press, the Ideal Home Exhibition publicity and advertisements for appliances and gadgets increasingly treated women as professional housewives, as not only managers of their homes but also workers. The new housekeeping and women's magazines educated the housewife in labour-saving ways and the application of scientific management techniques to her home. Rational housekeeping ideas rapidly became assimilated into the Daily Mail. In August 1919, for example, the Daily Mail published a diagram that showed how a well-planned kitchen could reduce the number of steps required to make afternoon tea from 350 to 50. Gadgets, especially those powered by electricity, were curiosities in the early 1920s. A photograph taken at the Ideal Home Exhibition and published in the Daily Mail in 1920, showing 'Electricity's Aids to the tea-table', used labels to identify the new electrical appliances on display.

In an attempt to win women over to new-fangled aids to housework, in February 1920 the Daily Mail gave an account of a party of fifty charwomen employed in Government offices ('there have been no sterner critics') who were taken by their employers to see labour-saving devices. The Daily Mail recounted how Mrs Holroyd, 'veteran of Whitehall', who had 'swept on for 43 years' and was now more than 70 'but still on active service', was a hard case to win over to the labour-saving cause, believing in the power of elbow-grease over such new notions. Mrs Holroyd declared: 'you don't get me messing about with electricity' and dismissed a demonstration of a patent vacuum cleaner as suitable for clean places such as bathrooms, but no good for dirty offices. She was finally persuaded to try her hand at a 'mechanical scrubber with brush and mop attached'. Another charwoman was brought in to demonstrate side by side the method which Mrs Holroyd had used all her life: *In a few minutes Mrs Holroyd was pushing the automatic scrubber with great relish and minimum exertion up and down the floor at Olympia... Mrs Holroyd remarked: 'Well, there may be something after all in these new-fangled ideas', and when she left she had a handful of catalogues.*

Below: The Royal Gardens at the 1922 Exhibition. Each of the ten gardens was designed by a member of royalty, including Queen Alexandra, the Queen of the Netherlands, the Queen of Spain, the Queen of Norway and the Queen of Belgium. The display was organised by Middlesex Hospital and the additional entrance fee of one shilling was devoted to furthering the hospital's work.

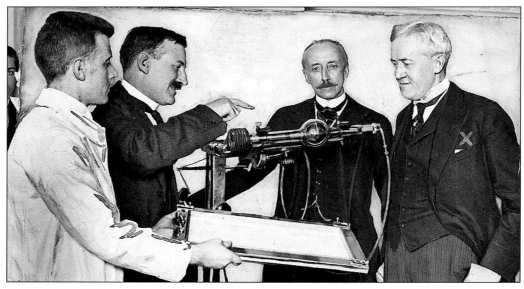

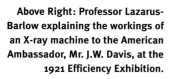

Above Right: Professor Lazarus-Barlow explaining the workings of an X-ray machine to the American Ambassador, Mr. J.W. Davis, at the 1921 Efficiency Exhibition.

Above: Advertisement from the 1922 Ideal Home Exhibition catalogue.

Below Left: Some of the fifty charwomen from Government offices watch Mrs Holroyd trying out a mechanical scrubber.

Below Right: A miniature immersion heater, which could heat a cup of water to boiling in 80 seconds, being demonstrated at the 1922 Exhibition.

The younger women were said to be especially full of appreciation. One declared that it was the first 'real treat' she had had for years and if only she had such a device, her hands would not be so bad - a complaint with which middle-class women readers would have sympathised.

THE DRIVE FOR NATIONAL EFFICIENCY

The Daily Mail was so convinced of the importance of national efficiency that in 1921 it temporarily replaced the Ideal Home Exhibition with the Daily Mail Efficiency Exhibition. The notions of labour-saving and progress in the workplace that the Efficiency Exhibition presented had much in common with those proposed by the Ideal Home Exhibition in the domestic sphere. The Efficiency Exhibition also focused on the disabled, as it was felt that those who had given so much for the war were owed the opportunity to participate fully in society through work. A display mounted by the Ministry of Labour, which took up the whole of the Olympia Annexe, showed disabled men working at forty different trades, and one of the more bizarre sights of the exhibition was that of disabled ex-servicemen with artificial limbs constructing the very arms that they themselves were using. Disabled men were also employed to build the stands, which, the Daily Mail declared, constituted 'an exhibition

before an exhibition' that demonstrated how well each man had been trained for the job.

The Daily Mail continued its efficiency drive in 1921 by building a model village to demonstrate the latest house-building techniques to local authorities. The village, at Welwyn Garden City in Hertfordshire, is now known as Meadow Green but was originally known as Dailymail.

Dailymail village, as a generous gift to the nation, was a useful form of publicity for the Daily Mail. During a single week of its construction in 1921, 3,000 people made the 35-minute journey from King's Cross to the site. This publicity had a high cost - in 1994 it was estimated that at present prices such a development would cost more than £5 million. For once, this stunt may not have actually displeased Northcliffe, who was a firm supporter of the Garden Cities Movement that had founded Welwyn Garden City in 1919. The village opened on 2 March, 1922 to coincide with the start of the Ideal Home Exhibition. A scale model of the village was on display in Olympia, but visitors were invited to make a special excursion to Welwyn Garden City.

Dailymail village consisted of 41 cottages, representing 16 different systems of housing construction, planned along Garden City lines. The specifications of the cottages made them eligible for state financial aid under the 1919 Housing Act and some of them were

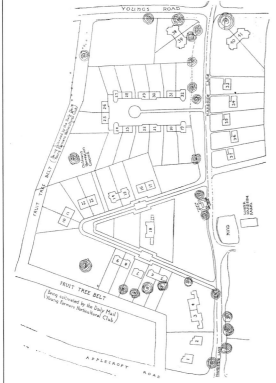

Above: Model of Dailymail Village, which was shown at the Ideal Home Exhibition.

Left: A plan of the village layout. Viscount Hampden, Lord Lieutenant of Hertfordshire, turned the first sod on the site on June 9th, 1920. The village was surrounded on one side by the Fruit Tree Belt, which was planted with a variety of fruit trees and bushes.
It was tended by the young residents of the district, who formed themselves into the first Daily Mail Young Farmers Horticultural Club. The Fruit Tree Belt was eventually eaten away, as residents began to include the ground into their gardens.

Above: A miniature scale model of a country house built in Bryscom building stone, with West Country stone tile roof and a 'Valley' patent hard tennis court in front. The display was part of the stand of Gilliam and Co., quarry owners and suppliers of garden stone, at the 1923 Exhibition.

Right: Bungalow Town under construction for the 1923 Exhibition.

Far Right: Bungalow Town, as seen from the gallery of the New Hall. The Ideal Home Exhibition had previously concentrated more on two-storey houses, but Bungalow Town was conceived in response to a perceived demand for the features of a two-storey house in a one-storey building. The Daily Mail ran a competition for a Labour-Saving Bungalow in 1923 and the winning designs were displayed on one of the stands in Bungalow Town.

left partly finished so that the construction methods could be appreciated. The cottages were modern not just in architectural style. Many of them featured new construction techniques developed during the war, such as a steel frame system and standardised components, and bathrooms and labour-saving devices were included.

With the exception of a flat-roofed, concrete 'Italian villa', which was 'a striking example of modern methods applied to classic design', the majority of houses were designed in a neo-Georgian style. The houses in the village were offered for sale after the Exhibition at prices ranging from just over £750 for a three-bedroom cottage to £2,100 for a four-bedroom Georgian-style home (now valued at around £200,000). Such prices made them affordable only to the middle classes.

In 1994 the Mail on Sunday's You Magazine visited Meadow Green to interview some of the current inhabitants of the Daily Mail houses, revealing their subsequent history. Most appear to have been altered or extended in some way to reflect shifting sets of ideals. For example, the 'Standardised Building' semis originally consisted of a ground floor with living room, parlour and kitchen, with three bedrooms and a bathroom above. One of the houses was first occupied by the Canossian Daughters of Charity, a teaching order based in Verona. They installed vast double doors between the living room and parlour to convert them into one large room for meetings, and one of the bedrooms was a consecrated chapel. The house was subsequently owned by Jack Catchpool, the first secretary of the Youth Hostel Association of England and Wales and later president of the international YHA. It was the international headquarters for the YHA and a focal point for hostellers from all over the world until Catchpool's death in 1970. The current owners, Catchpool's nephew and his wife, have extended the house to make a bigger kitchen and added a garage. Although Meadow Green may have lost some of its intended community spirit, a few of the current residents still appreciate the original design features of their houses that have survived. For example, the present inhabitants of the timber-framed Labour-saving Cottage (original cost £850, current value around £150,000) are very appreciative of features such as a laundry

Above: A housemaid's corner cupboard, which was featured in the Labour-Saving Section at the Exhibition in 1924.

Left: The Bolton double saucepan and kettle demonstrated at the 1926 Exhibition, one of a range of cooking utensils invented by Mrs Henry Bolton. It was designed to enable two saucepans and a kettle to fit over one gas burner, thus saving both space and gas.

chute enabling washing to be dropped from the lavatory into the kitchen, two serving-hatches in the kitchen and cupboards incorporated in the roof space.

The Daily Mail intended its 1922 ideal village to be an object lesson in efficiency. It gave work to ex-servicemen, who tested out the latest pre-fabrication building techniques on fully up-to-date labour-saving houses. As part of the drive for 'national efficiency', the 1922 Exhibition also featured a Children's Welfare section. The Exhibition continued to take an interest in child care throughout the inter-war years and the Exhibition's emphasis on the planning of the labour-saving ideal home also included the nursery.

SHOWING HOW OTHERS LIVE

One of the 1922 Ideal Home Exhibition's most reported exhibits was, however, a display of inefficiency: a Lanarkshire miner's cottage. Lord Northcliffe was sympathetic to the plight of the miners, who had gone on strike after a wage cut, and admired their fortitude. While touring the coalfields of Yorkshire, Lancashire and Lanarkshire (in his Rolls-Royce) in 1921, he decided that the dreadful houses the miners lived in were part of the cause of their unhappiness and strikes. He resolved to buy one of the hovels that the miners lived in and bring it to show at the next Ideal Home Exhibition.

A Lanarkshire miner's cottage was duly reconstructed at the Exhibition and visitors had a chance to observe the life of the miner and his family. Entering by the front door of the cottage and passing out by the coal-hole, inside they could see only two beds, one in which all the children but one slept, the other for the miner and his wife and the remaining child. They could observe the cottage's living inhabitants: Mr Moffat, a Lanarkshire miner, his wife and four children. Although many of the supposedly authentic living exhibits at exhibitions were, in fact, actors, in this case the miner and his family were really who they appeared to be. Following a newspaper report of the Ideal Homes retrospective exhibition at the Design Museum in 1993, which included archive photographs of the miner's cottage, Douglas Allen identified the people in the photographs as his Great-Grandfather and family who came from Watsonville. Photographs from their family album show Hugh Moffat and his family and a replica of their cottage at the Exhibition, and these had puzzled Mr Allen for some years. The presence of the miner gave the cottage a seal of authenticity. In his 'workaday' clothes and with a lamp slung around his neck, he answered questions on the life

Above: The Phonolamp, a decorative table lamp incorporating an electric gramophone in its base, from the 1923 Exhibition.

Right: The Lanarkshire Miner's Cottage at the 1922 Exhibition, a building that was 'the worst kind of human habitation in Great Britain' and 'in stark contrast to the other dwellings shown'.

of Lanarkshire miners proposed by a Daily Mail reporter. When asked if the cottage was the 'real thing', he replied that it was the 'real Mckay':

Some have wooden floors, because that's cheaper than repairing stone, and there's no back door. But it's very like the image, and there's plenty more like it where we come from.

Mrs Moffat demonstrated to astonished Daily Mail readers how she managed to cook, look after the children and keep the one-roomed cottage clean, 'despite the absence of kitchen and other equipment that the average housewife regards as essential to domestic management'.

Northcliffe was not convinced of the authenticity of the reconstruction:

The Miner's Cottage looks, of course, very comfortable indeed. It has electric light, which is rare in miners' cottages. It is a beautiful dry place and in many mining villages it rains nearly every day. There is no indication that there are no sanitary arrangements and the casual looker goes there and says 'How delightful'.

The presence of the cottage at the Exhibition provided a marker against which progress in home-making could be measured. Reports in the Daily Mail constantly contrasted the cottage with the modern housing found elsewhere in the Exhibition.

Below: Advertisement from the 1920 Exhibition catalogue, detailing the individual items available from Harrods to completely furnish a six-roomed flat for only £500.

Above: The Township of Ideal Homes under construction in the New Hall for the 1924 Exhibition. On the left is an ultra-modern house for £1,200, on the right a Georgian-style house for £1,100, and in the background a luxury £2,500 house with Tudor overtones in its design.

Right: The completed Township of Ideal Homes. The Tudor-style luxury house provided five bedrooms - one with an en suite dressing room - and included a servants' sitting room on the ground floor.

Above: The glamour and mystery of the East comes to the Exhibition in 1923, in the shape of Persian weavers making carpets by hand.

Left: The Duchess of York being shown round the Township of Ideal Homes after opening the Exhibition.

The post-war depression turned the attention of the Daily Mail and the Exhibition more towards home, and the representations of non-European peoples were largely absent from the Exhibitions of 1920 and 1922. Living displays of foreign peoples later appeared under the guise of the Home Industries section - for instance, in 1923 a display of Egyptian handicrafts was shown, with authentic Persian weavers making carpets. In 1925, a new section of the Exhibition showed craftsmen of many lands. In stands characteristic of their countries, peasant workers from Egypt, Australia, Poland, Palestine, Burma and all parts of the Orient worked on decorative items with their 'primitive tools'. The kind of decorative work they were doing has been and still is highly prized in England - rows of ebony elephants and Benares brassware are still displayed in many homes.

TEACHING THE ART OF LIVING

From 1923 onwards, the Ideal Home Exhibition was firmly fixed on the needs of its core audience and concentrated on the presentation of a constantly evolving and progressing new commercial culture of home-making. In effect, the modern housewife could never achieve her 'ideal home', because technology was constantly improving; each ideal was surpassed by another. Each Ideal Home Exhibition promised to surpass the previous one with its labour-saving innovations and the promise of improvement.

In 1924 the Exhibition catalogue declared:

The Daily Mail Ideal Home Exhibition is everybody's exhibition…For, dealing as it does with the art of home-making, the exhibition teaches the art of living. The two things are inseparable and folk in every walk of life are seeming more and more to realise, in the words of HM the King, that 'The foundations of the nation's greatness are laid in the homes of the people'.

One of the most popular displays at the Exhibition of 1925 was Queen Mary's Doll's House. Designed by Sir Edwin Lutyens, the Doll's House was a complete miniature mansion, 102 inches long, furnished and decorated in the style of a royal palace on a scale of one inch to a foot. A team including Princess Marie Louise, with well-known artists and designers, decorated the Doll's House in exquisite detail. The outside walls rose so that the detail of each room could be seen. The house offered visitors an opportunity to peek into the imagined domestic life of the royal family and was said to have greatly endeared Queen Mary to the nation. There was an extra admission fee of one shilling to see it, which raised £20,000 for charity.

The other memorable display was a remarkable full-size model of the Prince of Wales standing beside his horse in front of a typical Canadian homestead, all sculpted out of Canadian butter in a display of technical virtuosity. The Prince of Wales was incredibly popular; his travels through the Empire as a royal ambassador made the crown a living, not just formal, bond of Empire.

Above: Illustration of the exterior of Queen Mary's Dolls House. Its thirty-two rooms were all exquisitely furnished in miniature, even down to tiny Havana cigars on the desk in the library.

Right: The Hamlet of Heart's Desire, the display of houses at the 1925 Exhibition, was built around a village green with a small stream running through the centre crossed by stone bridges. The entire display was built in twenty-three days, including all the furnishing of the houses. The backdrop was a painted view of scenery inspired by the Cotswold hills.

DAILY MAIL IDEAL HOME EXHIBITION, OLYMPIA, 1926.
THE FRENCH KITCHEN

DAILY MAIL IDEAL HOME EXHIBITION, OLYMPIA, 1926.
THE DANISH KITCHEN

DAILY MAIL IDEAL HOME EXHIBITION, OLYMPIA, 1926.
THE SPANISH KITCHEN

The 1925 Exhibition also featured a display of six Ideal Boudoirs, including one designed by disabled ex-servicemen and another 'designed by a woman for woman's use'. Betty Joel, a self-taught designer who was very successful, used curved edges to her furniture to echo the feminine form, abolished all unnecessary mouldings and projections and introduced an innovative recessed drawer handle that she claimed reduced the number of surfaces that needed dusting. Women's magazines of the period praised her work, but it was not well received by the design press.

HOMES FROM THE PAST AND THE FUTURE

In 1926 F.R. Yerbury, Secretary of the Architectural Association and author of a series of books on modern architecture, created a display of Old Kitchens of the Nations at the Exhibition. The European countries in the display were Sweden, England, Spain, Holland, Denmark and France. He was also particularly interested in peasant design, so he included a kitchen from China, a country whose design was much admired by architects at the time. Each of the displays depicted a rural, traditional kitchen, from a non-specified time in the past. They were all rural, rather than urban, since, it was claimed, this meant they were not subject to change and remained timeless: although in the wider sphere of architecture one country might influence another, such external influences had no effect on remote cottages and isolated farmhouses. The Old English Kitchen breathed the very spirit of the English countryside as it was around one hundred years before, with brick floor and chintz-decked mantelpiece, pewter, brass and china ornaments, a grandfather clock, bed-warmer and a wide open fireplace with bread oven at one side. Yerbury was assisted by private individuals from each country, as well as the Danish Museum and a Dutch-run London shop.

Above: The photographs of each of the Old Kitchens of the Nations were issued as a series of postcards. In the catalogue the French Kitchen was characterised as being over-full of furniture, while the Danish Kitchen was noted as being very bright and gay. The Spanish Kitchen was described as typically being at the end of a courtyard or outer room, which would be used for storing farm implements or carts – hence the railings to divide the two areas. The American kitchen, shown bottom right, was displayed as a contrast to the others.

Right: Visitors admiring Queen Mary's Dolls House, which even had its own miniature garden.

Below: Princess Marie Louise being escorted through the Village of Open Doors at the 1926 Ideal Home Exhibition.

Opposite: The Village of New Ideas at the 1927 Exhibition. The show houses were always one of the most popular sections of the Exhibition and people queued for some time to see inside them.

Right: Overall view of the Main Hall at the 1926 Exhibition. In the centre in the background is the Fountain Court, over which looms an imposing bronze dome. Around the fountain, the Court of Fine Furniture displayed the latest furnishing ideas.

Below: The Tibbenham Tudor House in the 1926 Village of Open Doors. Its construction combined the traditional technique of half-timbering with the time-saving and durability of concrete. The basic wood framing was erected quickly and the gaps between filled with a double thickness of concrete divided by asbestos sheet. The speed of construction allowed the roof to be added within a few days, which meant that the remainder of the internal construction could be completed without regard to weather conditions.

Above: The Village of New Ideas at the 1927 Exhibition had as a backdrop gigantic sheets of scenery hung from the roof, painted with blue skies and mist-hung hills. The half-timbered Tudor Manor House on the left was the largest house ever built at the Exhibition, with six large bedrooms and a 24ft-long lounge. Next to it is a completely modern and labour-saving design by the Universal Housing Company, built of reinforced concrete with steel casement windows.

Far Left: An unusual piece of furniture from the 1929 Exhibition – an oak-framed settee, which could be quickly converted into a dining table.

Left: The shimmering white pylon above the extra gallery built at the end of the Main Hall for the 1927 Exhibition. The gallery contained the Terrace of Beauty, where mannequins displayed the wares of famous beauty product manufacturers.

Each kitchen was constructed in three dimensions, with a fireplace and working implements, and peopled with a 'native girl … at her duties' in 'appropriate national costume'. A stylised archway framed each scene, giving a picture postcard effect - the photographs were also issued as postcards. The display was contrasted with a modern American kitchen, designed by G.E.W. Crowe, which was displayed next to the old kitchens. This 'model of scientific arrangement' was not only planned to be labour-saving, but also illustrated the great changes in hygiene that had taken place and the possibilities opened up by the use of electricity.

The first House of the Future appeared at the Ideal Home Exhibition in 1928. Designed by S. Rowland Pierce and R.A. Duncan ARIBA, the house was built on a frame of hidden stainless steel supports. This frame would be covered with a tough material (which had not yet been invented) similar to horn, which could be cut and welded at high temperatures and would come in any colour or pattern desired. This material would form both the inner and outer walls, as well as the floors. Inside there was no staircase, only a lift, although there was an outside staircase to the flat roof.

Daily Mail
IDEAL HOME EXHIBITION

OLYMPIA · LONDON · W
FEBRUARY 28 ···
MARCH 24 · 1928

" *The foundations of the National Glory are set in the Homes of the People.*"
—*KING GEORGE V.*

Opposite: Advertisement for the Ideal Home Exhibition to be held in the year 2000, from the special edition of the Daily Mail that was published to celebrate the House of the Future in 1928.

Above: Title page from the 1928 catalogue. The quote by King George V was taken from a speech he had made to the Convocation of York on 8 July, 1910.

Left: The boudoir of Miss 1929, by designer Betty Joel, from the display of Bedrooms Through The Ages. With black enamelled walls and a polished copper ceiling, the room was both sitting room and bedroom. It was furnished with a cocktail cabinet and a combined radio-gramophone as well as the more usual bed and dressing table.

Above: The first House of the Future, one of the most daring and original homes in the Exhibition's history.

'A colour to suit the temperament' was the basis of the interior and even the lighting was in various colours. The kitchen was designed in long and compact lines, like a dining car, and disposable dishes, plates and cups were to be used so no washing-up was needed. Cooking and freezing were done by electricity. A table in the dining room could be folded and wheeled into the kitchen when necessary and easy chairs could be deflated and rolled up when they were not needed. The space of the house was as adaptable: two double bedrooms could be converted into four cabin-like bunk bedrooms with roller shutters. The beds could be heated by electrically-connected mattresses and heating throughout the house would come from electric panels on the floor. Its flat roof was topped with glass-covered pergolas for sunny days, while on dull days the occupants could retire to a bathing pool, lit by artificial sunlight, on the roof of the aero-car garage. Ultra-violet ray treatment was available throughout the house. It was a house not built to last a lifetime, but to become out of date as a car went out of date, and to be replaced in the same way.

The House of the Future had a futuristic garden that was quite unlike those of 1928. Instead of a wall, it had an arrangement that provided full or half shield against the wind. Water ran down the centre of the garden over tiles and could become, at the touch of a button on the house's central switchboard, a moving stream of fire. Flowers were packed tightly into oblong beds in cubist designs. The appearance of the garden could easily be changed by calling the public gardener, who could lift flowerbeds out in squares and replace them with squares in a different arrangement. Such a garden ran in stark contrast to the cottage ideal of the time and the construction of gardening as a leisure pursuit. The House of

the Future presented a fantasy of domestic life, where everyday household tasks would be automated.

A special edition of the Daily Mail was published, dated 1 January, 2000, to celebrate The House of the Future. The paper declared that the servant problem was at last conquered by the 'domestic labour eliminator', It forecast atomic energy, colour television and the Channel Tunnel, but deemed that inter-planetary space travel had not yet been achieved. The paper contained an advertisement for the 2000 Ideal Home Exhibition, held at an enlarged Olympia, which had parking space for 10,000 aeroplanes (there were so many private aero-cars that the sun was in danger of being blocked out). The women who flocked to the exhibition from all over the country and the Continent, it reported, could see cooks making concentrated foods containing all the essential vitamins.

The House of the Future was built within the Sunbeam Town. It was characteristic of the Ideal Home Exhibition to include a wide variety of styles side by side. The Sunbeam Town display consisted of eight houses of varying styles, including a simple Georgian house, an up-to-date Tudor-style home and the House of the Future. All the houses were designed to catch as much sunlight as possible, as at the time sunlight was believed to be very beneficial to the health. The concrete-built Sunshine Cottage had a flat roof combined with neo-Georgian details and the Sunbeam House, also made of concrete, was built in streamlined style. The two Tudorbethan houses, a style which was usually thought of as being dark because of its lattice windows, combined half-timbered external details with 'vita-glass' windows which were set to catch sunlight from every available angle throughout the day. A full page spread in the Daily Mail showed the extraordinary array of styles that made up the Sunbeam Town.

For the Exhibition of 1929, Yerbury organised a display of Bedrooms Through the Ages in which the bedchambers of women, from the cave of a primitive woman to the boudoir of Miss 1929, were reconstructed. The history of bedrooms was illustrated with a pre-historic cave, an Egyptian sleeping apartment, an Ancient Greek bedroom, a Japanese multi-purpose room, a richly decorated bedchamber from Renaissance Florence, a graceful eighteenth century French bedroom and a heavily furnished English Victorian room, ending with Betty Joel's modernistic design for the Bedroom of Today.

Above Left: To go with the House of the Future a futuristic car, which would also incorporate a boat and an aeroplane.

Above Right: One of the bedrooms in the House of the Future, each of which had cupboards and wardrobes - although they were not yet built-in.

ADVERTISERS' ANNOUNCEMENTS.　　SATURDAY, The Daily Mail FEBRUARY 18, 1928.　　ADVERTISERS' ANNOUNCEMENTS.

DAILY MAIL IDEAL HOME EXHIBITION
OLYMPIA · LONDON · W ··· FEBRUARY 28 ··· MARCH 24

NEW CONCRETE IDEAS.

Advantages of Prize-Winning House for £1,750.

The perspective of the winning design in Class A of the competition for architects, promoted by the Portland Cement Selling and Distributing Co., Ltd., is illustrated below. The house itself, at the Ideal Home Exhibition, is a striking object lesson in the use of concrete in domestic architecture.

The construction of this house is concrete throughout, with its walls, floors, roof and stairs built in situ. The whole of the interior is covered with an insulating material which gives a warm, sound finish, pre-

The interior has been kept clear of all dust-collecting mouldings, etc.; the doors throughout are of the flush type which have no panels or mouldings; the radiators likewise are of a smooth, easily cleaned hospital type. The accommodation provided in the house is as follows:

The hall (12ft. 0in. x 9ft. 0in.) has a tiled rubber floor which is quiet and easily cleaned. There is a small lavatory and w.c. off the hall.

The sitting-room (14ft. 0in. x 22ft. 6in.) has windows to both the front and back gardens and French casement windows leading out to the latter. The maple floor in this room makes it suitable for dancing.

The dining-room also has a maple floor and an electric fire.

The kitchen (14ft. 0in. x 11ft. 0in.) has been planned and furnished on modern lines with the most up-to-date labour-saving fitments, which include an electric refrigerator.

On the first floor are the four bedrooms and maid's room. Bedrooms Nos. 2 and 4 are 11ft. 0in. x 11ft. 8in., No. 5 is 11ft. 0in. x 10ft. 6in., and the maid's room is 10ft. 8in x 7ft. 3in. The best bedroom (15ft. 0in. x 11ft. 6in.) has French casement windows which open out on to a balcony. For the bathroom on this floor the most efficient sanitary fittings have been selected, including a hot towel rail, and all water taps, etc., are of a special easily cleaned type.

Erected by the Universal Housing Co., Ltd., Bury Works, Rickmansworth, Herts. Price for house, £1,750.

"Sunbeam House," the £1,750 Concrete House, erected by the Universal Housing Co., Ltd., Bury Works, Rickmansworth, to the prize-winning designs of Thos. S. Tait, F.R.I.B.A., 1 Montague-place, Bedford-square, London, W.C.1. Stand No. 38, New Hall, Olympia, London, W.

vents any dampness or condensation, and can be painted, distempered or papered.

The house is kept warm and free from draughts by a low-pressure water-heating system. Electrical power plugs are provided in all rooms.

THE "SUN-TRAP" HOUSE.

Sunshine Home Without a Single Dark Corner.

The A.M.A. Potters Bar "Sun-Trap" House has been designed to catch every moment of sunshine throughout the day in the principal room. It is glazed throughout with the well-known "Vita-Glass," the only glass manufactured which does not restrict the ultra-violet rays, so necessary to health.

The exhibit has been placed on an angle in order to derive the full advantage of views, and the presentation of three of its sides to the view from the entrance way thus provides great attractiveness.

The entrance loggia provides a quaint and very useful feature, and the hall is cut off from the staircase.

On the left of the hall is the dining-room—measuring 16ft. x 11ft. This room is panelled from picture rail to floor in Venesta Panelling, giving a Tudor effect. In addition to a large bay window, there is also a quaint niche window in this room placed to catch errant sunrays. On the right is the lounge, which measures 19ft. 11¼in. x 11ft. This room is also panelled with Venesta Panelling, finished grey-wood. In this room also there is a niche window.

Another doorway leads into the kitchen which is 11ft x 11ft. There is also, in addition, a large larder cupboard. The kitchen is also fitted with an enclosed dresser, a porcelain pantry sink 27in. x 16in. x 10in., and two draining boards. Between the lounge and the kitchen there is a toilet fitted with w.c. and lavatory basin.

On the first floor there are three bedrooms, as follows:—

No. 1, 17ft. x 11ft., having an oriel window and niche window.

No. 2 measures 13ft. x 11ft. with similar windows.

Bedroom No. 3, 11ft x 11ft., fitted with flue for gas fire and ample window space. All bedrooms are planned to take a double bed without crowding. On this floor there is a bathroom, w.c., and airing cupboard, and off the landing a very interesting feature is the covered-in balcony, of sufficient size to provide for alfresco meals, or for sleeping out in summer.

All rooms and ceilings are square. It is claimed there is not a dark corner in the house.

The house, as shown at Olympia, designed by Mr. W. J. King, architect, 5, Great James-street, Bedford-row, W.C.1 (in whom the copyright of the design is vested), could be erected on a level site in most districts for £1,350. Included stoves and sanitary fittings as exhibited. "Vita-Glass" is included at a small extra cost.

The A.M.A. Potters Bar "Sun-Trap" House, erected by A.M.A. Portable and Permanent Building Works, Ltd., High-road, Laindon, Essex. Designed by W. J. King, 5, Great James-street, Bedford-row, W.C.1. Stand No. 35, New Hall, Olympia, London, W.

SIMPLE GEORGIAN HOUSE.

Fine Old Marble Mantelpieces in Living Rooms.

The leisurely and spacious period of Queen Anne and the early Georges was the inspiration of this charming house, which has all the dignity and stability allied with comfort of typical houses of the period.

The external walls are faced with purple bricks, giving the mellowing effect of time, and forming a setting for the characteristic pine doorway with its elegant Corinthian columns,

All external woodwork is painted a rich cream, thus giving the right touch to the architectural effect. The completed whole gives a picture of a "home" restful and charming which must appeal to all.

The interior of the house comes fully up to expectations. There is on the ground floor a dining-room, 24ft. 6in. long x 13ft. 6in. broad ; on the opposite side of the hall is a lounge of equal proportions restful in its decorations and furniture.

The charm of these two rooms is greatly enhanced by fine antique marble mantelpieces recently removed from a well-known Georgian residence.

In the centre of the house is a large square hall and a typically broad and easy Georgian staircase, with solid newels, shaped ramps and thick turned balusters, leading to the upper floor.

The whole accommodation on the ground floor has the spacious comfort our forefathers wisely demanded for their reception rooms.

The same air of comfort pervades the bedrooms, which, five in number, are all arranged on the one floor. They are all roomy and spacious and offer every facility for the furnisher's art.

"Sundour" fadeless fabrics are being used throughout. The furnishing has been carried out with every consideration for the best effect, at the lowest possible price consistent with quality.

The house complete with kitchen offices and servants' quarters would cost approximately £5,000.

The "Sundour" House, erected by Maple and Co., Ltd., Tottenham Court-road, W. 1. Stand No. 36, New Hall, Olympia, London, W.

supports and scrolled and pedimented overdoor.

The windows are of good size with exposed and moulded frames divided with stout sash bars into proportionate square, thus keeping the scale of the house, which large sheets of plate glass inevitably destroy.

The house is crowned with a bold overhanging modillion cornice and a broad expanse of red tiled roof. There are quaint arched recesses over the entrance door, with plastered backs.

WONDERS OF SUNBEAM TOWN.

Where Science Has Helped to Make Healthful, Sunshine Houses.

Fresh Progress in Home Planning.

SUNSHINE-SAVING is to be a prominent feature of "Sunbeam Town," the Housing Section of the "Daily Mail" Ideal Home Exhibition, which will be opened at Olympia on Tuesday, Feb. 28th, by the Rt. Hon. The Lord Mayor and Lady Mayoress of London.

In each of the picturesque cluster of houses —completely erected, equipped and furnished— which make up "Sunbeam Town" every effort has been made to ensure that in every room the maximum benefit of the sun's health-giving rays will be enjoyed.

Moreover, in a number of the houses, provision has even been made for the supply of artificial sun-light when King Sol proves niggardly in his attentions.

With sunlight-conservation as a common ideal, the houses, as will be seen by reference to the description in this page, are, nevertheless, widely varied in design and style.

They range from a simple wooden bungalow to the almost startling "House of the Future," described below. And, in every house there will be found new ideas for the beautifying and betterment of the home, which the visitor will be able to study at leisure.

"Sunbeam Town" is aptly named. Its rural atmosphere and charming setting will bring a delightful foretaste of summer to all who spend interested hours in surveying it.

It is, in itself, a complete exposition of modern housing—yet it represents only a small part of the ever-popular exhibition which occupies the eight acres of Olympia's floor space.

In the Main Hall, the Galleries and the Annexe, many surprises are in store for those who have visited the exhibition during its previous great successes. They will find what is to all intents and purposes a new exhibition in a new Olympia.

Great artistry has been employed, and notably dignified effects have been achieved, by the architects—Messrs. Tanner and Horsburgh of Birmingham.

A wonderful transformation has been effected in the erection of the Bridge of Beauty, which spans the Main Hall. This feature, built in imposing style, is the setting for a score or so of stands of special attraction for the modern woman.

Close to it is the Furniture Section set about a graceful fountain court. Here will be seen a wonderful display of rooms set out by the leading furnishing firms in styles old and new.

Towering above the exhibits in the Main Hall is the Eastern Bandstand—an imposing feature constructed of brass beautifully engraved and inset with rich colour.

The west end of the Main Hall represents the facade of a lovely old Georgian house on each side of which a graceful stairway leads to the Gallery where is the fascinating demonstration of British resources made by the Empire Marketing Board.

Beyond, the scent of flowers and the mellow glow of artificial sunlight will beckon the visitor to the Gardens of the Poets, where the finest landscape gardeners in the country have excelled themselves with the words of classic and modern poetry to inspire them.

A Cascade Tea Garden here will provide a delightful sanctuary for rest and refreshment.

Beauty there is in abundance at this wonderful exhibition, and, as is proper, utility is emphasised also. In the 400 exhibits of the exhibition there is to be seen almost everything that a year's scientific and mechanical progress has produced for greater home comfort.

In the fascination of its novelty, the allurement of its beauty and the richness of its interest—the Twelfth Daily Mail Ideal Home Exhibition is without doubt the brightest and best exhibition of the year.

THE HOUSE OF THE FUTURE.

An Architect's Daring Prophecy.

Of the many striking features which have, from time to time, lent special interest to the *Daily Mail* Ideal Home Exhibition, none has been so daring in idea and execution as the House of the Future.

This amazing house will excite wonder in all who look upon its strange factory-fashioned architecture.

Designed by Mr R A Duncan of Percy Tubbs, Son and Duncan, and erected by Bovis, Ltd., it is the materialisation of an architect's dream of the mass-production home of many years hence.

Literally a leap into the future it is the first serious attempt made to enable people to skip perhaps half a century and live for an hour surrounded by the things to which scientific progress is leading us.

Inevitably this daring foretaste of the future will result in controversy; but in doing so it will provoke thought and that is the object of its exhibit.

The following are a few of the out-standing features of what is, undoubtedly, the most interesting exhibit ever seen at Olympia.

A substitute is used to suggest a material never before employed—a thin, horn-like, impervious substance —carried by hidden supports of stainless steel.

The windows open and shut by rising and falling like a motor-car

An impression of "The House of the Future," one of the remarkable new features of the Ideal Home Exhibition. Erected by Bovis, Ltd., from the designs of Mr. R. A. Duncan, A.R.I.B.A., of Percy Tubbs Son and Duncan, 39, Great James-street, Bedford-row, London, W.C. 1. Stand No. 37, New Hall, Olympia, London, W.

window-screen, or by winding vertically like the windows of a limousine. All are closed at night. Oxonised air is carried to a ventilator over each bed.

Four of the bedrooms are like steamship cabins, but can be converted by means of roller shutters into two double-bedrooms. Heating is by means of electric panels in the floors. Beds are heated by electrical blankets. All the living rooms face the garden and the sun. Movable shutters enable study, living room and dining room to be opened up into one big L-shaped room for entertaining.

There is a bathing pool on the roof of the aero-car garage. Artificial sunlight and ultra-violet ray treatment are "on tap" throughout the house.

The British Thomson-Houston Company, Ltd., are laying 2½ miles of cable in the house and wiring 1,000 "Mazda" lamps.

The kitchen is long and compact like that of a railway dining-car. Easy chairs are pneumatic and can be deflated, rolled up and put away when not needed.

Down the centre of the garden water runs over tiles, and at the touch of an electric lighting button becomes like a living stream of fire. The whole of the flat roof of the house is occupied by pergolas covered with sunlight glass.

It is a house not built to last for centuries, but only until such time as progress makes it or any of its parts out-of-date. Then renewal, it is said, is merely a matter of ordering a new model or new part—just as you would in the case of a motor-car!

BUILDING MADE EASY.

Timber and Asbestos System.

This spacious Bungalow of attractive appearance containing an excellent living-room, three bedrooms, kitchen, bathroom and w.c., which is specially designed to accommodate those who require an inexpensive yet comfortable home, has much to commend it.

The exterior appearance is greatly enhanced by the ample oversail of the roof and two large, pleasing bay windows.

The interior is lined and ceiled with asbestos sheets, with battens forming panels. Walls can be either painted, papered, or distempered.

The walls are in complete sections of stout well-seasoned deal framing at about 3ft. centres, well cut and housed together, covered externally with lower part 1in. planed steam-proof weather-boards, upper part asbestos sheets with battens over joints, and fitted with doors and windows with all necessary fittings, also asbestos sheets to line interior.

Partitions as above covered one side with asbestos sheets and battens, also lining of the same material.

Roof of strong purlins resting on principals and hips, with best tongued and grooved matching, bitumen roofing, and red diagonal asbestos tiles to cover same.

Floor of strong stages, joists and best planed tongued and grooved floor boards.

The bungalow is sold complete and ready for fixing including: asbestos, joists and battens for flat ceilings, glass for windows, gutters and down pipes, and all external exposed woodwork treated with preservative.

This bungalow is supplied in sections, etc., convenient for handling, and ready for erection at the attractively low figure o. £172 10s. complete, delivered carriage paid to customer's nearest station in England or Wales. For stations in Scotland, Ireland or Channel Islands a slight extra charge is made.

The building is completely finished in the manufacturer's workshops to minimise the cost of erection, which can be done by local labour with ease.

The "Sunview" Bungalow exhibited by C. Albert and Company, 187, Brixton-hill, London, S.W. 2. Stand No. 40, New Hall, Olympia, London, W.

GARAGE IN THE HOUSE.

Attractive Home Planned for the Owner-Driver.

A House and Garage all under one roof is the novel plan of the C.S.A. Solar House. The combination of the two buildings gives an interesting and spacious house plan, an attractive front with the advantage of a warm garage.

Porch, lobby, and lavatory are all well arranged, and the hall is large and well lighted, with oak floor. Off the hall is a coat cupboard and the staircase is arranged as a central feature. The drawing-room, 17ft. 6in x 12ft. 6in., with a recessed fireplace, is a good apartment, and the dining-room close to kitchen, a square room with a good serving-space around table.

A labour-saving kitchen and a good larder and offices complete the house accommodation on the ground floor.

Then the garage with ample space for car and a recess to take a bench, a joy to the owner-driver, who has a taste for "tinkering."

On the first floor there are three good double rooms, and a fourth for maid. All rooms as well arranged for furniture and lighting.

A bathroom of ample size with Marsite marble lined walls and cased-in bath is a feature of the house, heated linen cupboard and, what is often forgotten, a good large boxroom, on the roof, but off the landing.

The house has been finished to save labour, the staircase with oak nosing and cork carpet treads saves that expensive item the stair carpet, with its annoying rods and continual brushing. Gas is used for heating the dining-room, the stove being set in a brick surround.

A coal fire for cheerfulness, with an especially attractive stone mantel, is installed in the drawing-room.

An independent boiler gives an efficient hot-water supply.

To obtain freedom from damp and noise, and to ensure an even temperature throughout the year, this house has an interior lining of Celotex insulating and Sound-deadening board, which is made of woven sugar-cane

The "Solar" House, erected by the Country Service Association, Ltd., Westmorland House, 127/131, Regent-street, W. 1. Designed by A. H. Jones, F.R.I.B.A. Stand No 42, New Hall, Olympia, London, W.

fibre, the strongest fibre known. The exterior walls are of 11in. hollow brick with stucco finish.

This house should appeal to those who are looking for a comfortable well-designed home, where everything has been considered to save labour and expense. Price £1,800.

£750 CONCRETE HOUSE.

Winning Design in Architects' Competition.

The exhibit illustrated below is built from the design which secured first place in Class B of the competition for architects promoted by the Portland Cement Selling and Distributing Co., Ltd.

It will be generally conceded that the author of Class B design have successfully arrived at a solution whereby the smallest house can be built of concrete—concrete in construction and concrete in principle.

"Sunshine Cottage," the £750 Concrete House erected by The Universal Housing Co., Ltd., Bury Works, Rickmansworth, Herts. In the prize-winning designs of Frank J. Brown and J. H. Peek, 50. Moorgate, London, E.C. 2. Stand No. 39, New Hall, Olympia, London, W.

The plan in its simplicity of arrangement has been developed on labour-saving principles—so essential in these days of domestic economy

The ground floor contains a comparatively large living room with a square sitting room—both leading off the main hall.

The kitchen scullery is well equipped to meet the needs of the modern housewife.

The upper floor contains one large bedroom with two well-proportioned smaller bedrooms.

The lavatory accommodation provides for a complete bathroom with bath that appeals in the treatment of the exterior design, and likewise much that will arouse criticism. The design in a new phase of thought and fully expresses the material used in the construction thereof.

The exterior walls are of mass concrete with well prepared shuttering to give a "dragged" effect to the external surface. The whole of the interior is covered with an insulating material which gives a warm, sound finish, prevents any dampness or condensation, and can be painted, distempered, or papered.

The roof and first floor are of concrete slab construction with light steel reinforcement.

The partitions are of breeze concrete slab formation and plastered.

The floors of living room, sitting room and bedrooms are finished with pine boarding on good grounds incorporated in the concrete bed.

All other areas of flooring are finished with approved patent joint-less flooring.

The walls are of standard cottage type—metal casements to open out.

The covering to roof construction of asphalt dressed over into gutters formed in the concrete.

Hot-water service is provided in scullery and bathroom. Price for house, £750.

SUN-BATHS FOR ALL.

Novel Features of Up-to-Date Tudor-Style Home.

"Vita-Glass" windows, a cleverly fitted sun-bathroom on the first floor and a sun parlour on the ground floor are special features of the "Sun-Bath" House.

Of attractive Tudor design externally, the house contains on the ground floor a large hall 12ft. 6in. x 10ft. 6in. tastefully panelled in oak; lounge 22ft. 0in. x 15ft. 6in., well lighted and with commodious ingle-nook, and from this room the sun-parlour is entered with its tiled floor, perfect ventilation, and lighted on two sides with "Vita-Glass."

The dining-room is 15ft. 0in. and also communicates with the sun-parlour and the hall; it is conveniently situated from a labour-saving point of view, well lighted and ventilated, and is served from the kitchen through an unobtrusive serving door.

Much care and consideration have been given to the kitchen in the "Sun-Bath" House. Every possible modern appliance is provided. The usual offices are suitably placed and correspond favourably with the general plan. There is a good larder, coal store, lavatory and w.c., the latter opening off a good-sized vestibule adjoining the front entrance door.

The first floor is reached from the hall by the well-planned staircase, and terminates on the landing, which is formed into a most attractive balcony surrounding and commanding a view of the hall below. There are five bedrooms, of varying sizes, to suit all requirements, these being well lighted and ventilated, and fitted with electric and other convenient appliances, including heating from a central system.

All these bed chambers open on to the balcony, which in turn communicates with the "sun-bathroom," this being carefully fitted with all requirements recommended by the medical profession to secure the most healthful advantages of sunlight under comfortable conditions.

Ample sanitary accommodation is provided on this floor.

The "Universal Sun-Bath" House, erected by The Universal Housing Company, Ltd., Bury Works, Rickmansworth, Herts. Stand No. 41, New Hall, Olympia, London, W.

The "Sun-Bath" House possesses many other advantages and is the outcome of building experience covering many years.

The cost being £1,975—ready for occupation—it comes within the reach of people of moderate means.